LESSONS FOR STEVIE

David Muensterman

Balboa Press books may be ordered through booksellers or by contacting:

Balboa Press
A Division of Hay House
1663 Liberty Drive
Bloomington, IN 47403
www.balboapress.com
1 (877) 407-4847

ISBN: 978-1-5043-2847-0 (sc)
ISBN: 978-1-5043-2848-7 (e)

Library of Congress Control Number: 2015903054

Print information available on the last page.

Balboa Press rev. date: 07/24/2015

BALBOA
PRESS
A DIVISION OF HAY HOUSE

I would like to thank Balboa press for the opportunity to turn a dream into a book.

To all of the people that have showered me with love and kind words for these lessons, thank you.

Dan Gieschen, thank you for a beautiful tribute and web page. Your friendship is something that I cherish so very much.

Margaret Pesa, my amazing editor and so much more. Words alone will never express the gratitude I have for you. The confidence I have in myself today is a direct reflection of the growth you made me see in myself. I may not have known it at the time, but that long drive through Africa would bless me with a friendship that I will forever measure the purest definition of that word.

Natalie, the strength you live your life by is infectious. The moment I laid my eyes on you, my life took on a whole new meaning. You are a shining example of someone who innately posseses the qualities these lessons embody. Thank you for the two most amazing gifts I will ever receive. What an awesome life we share.

Briggs, Daddy is so blessed to call you his son. You completed our family and everyday you teach me more and more. I love you Briggs.

Lastly, Stevie. You taught me what it was to truly look in the mirror. Your gifts fill my world with awe and wonder. Thank you for being you and honoring me with the best title I have ever had, your Daddy.

Lesson #1: Always Love Who You See In The Mirror!

This lesson is for Daddy, Stevie.

When Mommy and Daddy decided it was time to turn our relationship into a family, he had no clue what that entailed. All he knew was you were going be a lot of work and there would be no monetary compensation. Anyone who knows Daddy would say that equation was a recipe for disaster. The truth is that you are a lot of work, but that is only part of the story.

Lesson #2: Daddy, She Is Your Responsibility

Single Mommies and Daddies, how do you do it?

Stevie, the facts are that you sleep very little. You eat all the time. You use the diaper like you are trying to set a Guinness world record. You cannot do anything for yourself. Sometimes you cry and Daddy does not know why! You are fed - check. Clean diaper - check. Burped - check. Well rested - check. Daddy is holding, rocking, humming to you – check, check, CHECK! Why are you still upset? Daddy put in all this work and there is no paycheck, vacation, or sick day. But saying all that, the benefits outweigh the costs. He is so exhausted, but this is the best job in the world.

Daddy is excited about POOP! He broadcasts endless smiles a day because of you and feels love which grows exponentially everyday. You are DADDY'S responsibility. He wants to provide for you, feed you, clothe you, keep you safe, entertain you, teach you, and love you. For you Stevie, he will do this free of charge for as long as you need, and if he has his way, even longer.

Stevie, you can lay your head on Daddy's chest for comfort, to sleep, to cry, to laugh, when you do not feel well, or to talk in your own little language.

Lesson #3: This Parking Spot Will Always Be Open

Daddy is writing this down so it is public record -- this spot will always be available anytime you need it because the weird thing is that he needs it too.

Lesson #4: You Have To Trust In Life

There is nothing to be afraid of because if you truly trust, life will always support you. Sometimes you have to let go, have the confidence to take the next steps and believe the end result will net you what you want. Today, you went swimming. You just trusted you would be okay even though it was the first time you were in the ocean. You splashed around and knew you were being supported. Just like Mommy and Daddy were there today, we will be there every step of the way as we teach you to trust in yourself and to trust that life will always bring you what you need.

Lesson #5: Find Your Passion

No matter what it is that you want to do, BE PASSIONATE! When you find that passion, let it become part of you, and share it with the world.

P.S. If you want to help Daddy with the sharks that would be pretty cool.

Lesson #6: Live Your Dreams

Surround yourself with people who believe in your dreams. Let your imagination create the greatest worlds and fill them with everything that brings you joy. Feel the happiness that brings you closer to yourself. Dream BIG! Dreams do come true. How does Daddy know? Because he is going to go play in the ocean and call it work? No, it is because Daddy is looking at you.

Lesson #7: Find Your Laugh

Stevie, you are already pretty good at it, but find your laugh!

Let it start from your toes and race all the way out of your mouth. Let it be loud, funny, cute, long, deep, or even annoying. Who cares! Let it be yours. The best laughs are the ones that people know without seeing, or the ones that are contagious and get passed on to others. No matter what is going on in your life being able to laugh will always make things better. It is the best medicine.

Lesson #8: Do Not Ever Be Afraid To Speak Your Mind

Be sure of yourself and your beliefs. Do not be afraid to speak. Your voice counts just as much as the next person's. Your opinions do matter. Your perspective could be the one that clarifies an issue. Ask questions if you need answers. Conversely, your answers to questions are just as relevant as the person standing next to you. Stevie, you are smart and your outlook is impressive. Always stand up for what you believe.

Lesson #9: More Than Just a Name

Stevie, you were named after a man with whom Daddy did not spend enough time with while he was alive. We lost your Grandpa Steve before you were born. What Daddy can tell you about him was that he had a booming voice and a very warm smile. Your Mommy will one day tell you great stories about Grandpa Steve. But when Mommy was young, the relationship she had with Grandpa Steve was not ideal.

Mommy looked deep inside herself and saw how much she needed and wanted a deeper relationship with Grandpa Steve. They both loved each other, but there was no true father/daughter bond. She did an easy thing which can also be the hardest thing to do - she forgave both him and herself for their shortcomings. Grandpa Steve was a man who had a few flaws, but always faced his imperfections. With help from your Mommy, Grandpa Steve was able to work on some of these weaknesses and turn them into strengths. Through this work, he was able to become the Father that Mommy always wanted.

Daddy knows that Grandpa Steve is looking down at you and his mustache is smiling with love, and his affectionate and caring eyes are beaming with pride. Always be proud of your name, Stevie, because it is more than a name. It is a tribute to a great man who left us way too soon. Yet it also should remind you that sometimes we should not give up on people. With a little love and faith, relationships can be harmonious.

Lesson #10: Live In The Moment

As an older parent, there have been times Daddy wishes he could go back in time and be more in the moment. Then he remembers that those moments have passed, and all he needs to do is be present in this moment. Everything is happening now! Live and love life everyday, Stevie. See the beauty in the biggest, but more importantly, the smallest miracles that happen daily.

Beauty surrounds you all the time if you are present and looking for it. Everyday there are these precious moments that make living so easy to love - from seeing an old couple holding hands (no, not Mommy and Daddy!) to feeling a cool breeze on your cheek. The best part is if you do miss one of these moments it is okay, because another one will be coming very, very soon.

Lesson #11: There Are Days That Will Not Be Sunny

You will have days that will not go as planned. When things go awry, as they sometimes will, do not be afraid to start the day over. If you really look at what is bothering you, ask yourself if the issue is worth being upset about. Daddy bets that ninety percent of the time you will see your sadness can be turned around as quickly as it got there.

Change your thinking around the subject that is troubling you and your perspective will shift. Also, a big smile and a deep breath go a long way. You can always come to Daddy – he will always have a smile to counteract your blues.

Lesson #12: Stick With Your Friendships

Stevie, always care for your friends and nurture those relationships. Great friends are always good for a laugh, a shoulder and a secret. They are the ones that will stick up for you and love you through all the different waves of life. One thing to remember is to not change who you are to make certain people care. Good friends will always love you for who you are – eccentricities, clumsiness and all!

Sometimes people will come into your life who will make you second guess yourself or make you feel bad about you. Stevie, you will learn who to surround yourself with and sometimes you will have to say goodbye to people which may be very difficult. Remember Lesson #1? Always love who you see in the mirror. If any person ever makes you question the good things you see in the mirror, you should probably let that person go. Trust in who you see in the mirror, and as long as you love what is looking back, you will always thrive. The friendships you make along the way will only accentuate the person in that mirror.

Lesson #13: Be Fearless

One of Daddy's favorite quotes is from the movie Shawshank Redemption:
"Fear will hold you prisoner. Hope can set you free."

Daddy lived a lot of his life in fear. It was not until he faced those fears that he was really able to love and start living. This all goes back to…Lesson #1. There will be times when you look in that mirror, and you will be scared or confused. SEE it, FEEL it, UNDERSTAND it, WORK on it, and OVERCOME the fears. Sometimes these fears will go away quickly. Some will take a bit more time, but the sooner you face them, the sooner you will be free. Then there are those times when you have to have faith, and let that worry go. No fear will ever control you if you do not allow it to take over your life. Mommy and Daddy will always be there to help you overcome your obstacles if you ask.

Lesson #14: There Will Always Be People Who Have More Than You (And That Is Okay!)

There will also always be people who have a lot less than you. Never take for granted what you do have in your life. Always be thankful for all of your blessings.

You really do not need much to be happy. The best thing about having a heart full of love is it does not matter what you have or do not have in that moment. With a heart full of love, you have everything you need.

Lesson #15: Choose Your Words Carefully

There are lots of people who will teach you so much more than Daddy can if you just open your eyes and see the lesson. The word "retard" or "retarded" is used in such a common way now it is disturbing. Stevie, as you get older, choose your words carefully because even a word said in the most innocent way can hurt someone else.

Daddy cannot wait for you to meet your Uncle Bryan. Daddy's brother has taught him more about curiosity than any cat, more about excitement than any last second field goal, and more about innocence then any newborn baby. Stevie, your Uncle Bryan watches every Cubs game like it is the seventh game of the World Series. Uncle Bryan was in his late teens, and still could not wait for Santa Claus and the Easter Bunny to arrive. And Daddy will never forget Freddy. Freddy was Uncle Bryan's best friend. Freddy would come by to visit everyday. Your Grandpa and Grandma did not like Freddy because he would poke holes in all the screens trying to say "Hi" to Uncle Bryan. See Stevie, Freddy was a crow. Yes, Daddy said a crow! You had to see the friendship between Freddy and Uncle Bryan to believe it. Your Uncle Bryan is always into something or another. The one thing Daddy can guarantee is there will never be a dull moment when you hang out with your Uncle Bryan.

Uncle Bryan and the mentally challenged community have taught Daddy so much. They are perfection. They are in their purest state, always. Uncle Bryan is one of Daddy's greatest teachers. He has taught Daddy that being unique is a blessing. He has taught Daddy how to be patient and understanding, and most of all how to love unconditionally. We are all human, Stevie. We all feel pain when others say hurtful things to us, even if they are not doing it consciously. Everyone wants to be treated with the same dignity and respect, so choose your words with care.

Stevie, all of these lessons come from years of Daddy making mistakes, and then growing and learning about who he is and how he wants to live in the world. Talking with a very special friend the other day made him realize how many times he has pushed his feelings aside because he was too scared of confrontation. Daddy is definitely more self-aware now, however old habits can creep up from time to time. By writing this down for you, Daddy hopes to help himself as well.

Lesson #16: Stand Up For Yourself

If your feelings are being hurt, be assertive and express your own needs and wants. Your feelings matter just as much as anybody else's. You may not always get what you want, but at least you will feel like you took care of yourself.

Now, with this lesson comes another one!

Lesson #17: Know Your Role In The Situation

Are you being unfair in the situation? Are your expectations too high? Have you been honest about what happened? Once you realize your part in the situation, you can have an open and respectful interaction with the intended person and make sure your feelings are heard.

Stevie, above all, always remember to keep your values, self-respect and self-worth held to the highest of standards regardless of how people interact with you.

Lesson #18: Be A Kid

When you are young, Stevie, all you are going to want is to be older. It is kind of ironic that this is Lesson 18, the age when you are first considered an adult. Life happens so fast and you will not understand this because when you are a child time seems to go so slow.

Be a kid, Stevie! Be wide eyed at things you see for the first time. Make mistakes. Try lots of new things. Get dirty. Play pretend. Be carefree. Go outdoors. Get excited. Do everything a kid should do! Live and love life with the innocence which only a child possesses. You are only a child once, and for such a short time. You will be an adult for a long time. Whenever you want to be a grown-up, come to Daddy and we will play make believe. Daddy still likes being a kid!

Lesson #19: Figure Out What Is Really Important In Life

Daddy thought the most exciting part of today was going to be watching the football game. But you and Mommy had other plans.

Daddy got to feed you for the first time today. What an amazing experience to hold you and feed you. You just stared at Daddy and made him realize what is truly important. That does not mean that Daddy does not love football, but there are other things that he now values more than watching a game. Life is constantly changing and things change in importance. Go with the flow Stevie, so you do not miss out on what is really important.

Daddy did not pay much attention to this lesson until you were born.
Practicing it has brought him so much joy and peace.

Lesson #20: Slow Down

We get so busy in our everyday lives, with so much STUFF we think is important - work, bills, housework, chores, errands, television (oh, that is a big one), and so on. All this STUFF does matter, but it will also always be there. *SO SLOW DOWN, DADDY!*

Daddy meant to say SLOW DOWN, STEVIE… this is your lesson, right? Trying to fit you into all of Daddy's STUFF was so hard, and then it hit him. The most amazing thing that has ever happened to him - and he is trying to fit you in? What kind of mixed up priorities was Daddy living by?

Daddy's promise to you is that every chance he has, we will go and watch the sunset. It is our family time. It is the best thirty minutes of his day. During these moments, the only thing that matters is our family. It gives us a chance to talk, laugh, share, cry, think, love, reflect, or just sit and be still. Daddy treasures our sunsets. Stevie, when you get older and life is going too fast, find your sunset, whatever that may be. One last thing, sunsets happen everyday, and no matter how old you are, Daddy will always sit and enjoy them with you.

Stevie, today is a fun and easy lesson as long as you are always honest with yourself.

Lesson #21: Be True To Who You Are

This lesson will most likely take many forms in your life. You will find new things to learn and explore. You will have new loves and passions. There will also be times of confusion and uncertainty. As long as you stay true to yourself, you will always get the most out of life, even in more difficult times. What Daddy means by this, Stevie, is always do what you believe is right for you. Dress the way you want to dress. Dance the way you want to dance. Laugh at what you find funny. Cry when you are sad. LOVE the way YOU want to love. No matter what others may say or do, as long as you are true to who you are and you are honest with yourself, then all of the joys will be amazing, and all of the lows will be manageable. Every Lesson seems to lead back to Lesson #1: Love and Be Kind To The Person You See In The Mirror.

P.S. Did you know that Daddy painted his nails and had blue hair for many years? Please just warn Mommy if you decide to dye your hair all the different colors of the rainbow!

Lesson #22: Santa Claus Is Real!

Hopefully, this lesson will not have any meaning to you for many years. Some parents might even disagree with Daddy about this lesson. He is here to tell you that Santa Claus, The Easter Bunny, The Tooth Fairy – they are ALL real! Frosty and Rudolph? REAL! They are all real, Stevie, for as long as you believe in and need them. At some point, you might hear the opposite, but listen to Daddy! As long as you allow yourself to believe, they will all be here for you. As you get older, you may leave them for a while and say your Daddy did not tell you the truth, but he did.

Thanks to you Stevie, Daddy can tell you he saw Santa yesterday for the first time in a really long time. It was like Daddy was a child again. There was Santa sitting with Mrs. Claus and Daddy could not wait to put you in Santa's lap! It was good to see an old friend after all this time. As long as you allow yourself to believe Stevie, it is amazing what the truth really can be.

Five more days until your first Christmas, Stevie! Most people act endearingly different during the holiday season. People give more of themselves to others, laugh more and experience increased joy. Any family differences are set aside or at least are given a time out. The holidays are such an amazing time of year and they go by so fast.

Lesson #23: Always Remember the Spirit of Christmas

When we lose the holiday spirit, Stevie, it is just that we forgot what it is really about. Daddy will not lie, presents are wonderful, but they are the smallest part of Christmas. The holiday spirit encompasses many forms: a smile at a stranger, walking through snow looking at houses lit with bright lights, a little baby in her first Christmas outfit.

There are so many things we do during the holidays which we ignore the rest of the year. We are more inclined to strengthen relationships, establish family traditions, and volunteer and give more resources to those less fortunate.

Daddy is going to try to take this lesson and carry it on after the holidays. You are going to help remind him to keep this lesson alive all year. Every time a stranger smiles at you, or says how beautiful you are, he will smile back and say thank you. *Gratitude.* Every time a family member calls to see how you are, Daddy will pick up or call back. *Respect.* And every time you make Daddy laugh, he will hold on to what really matters and let the small stuff slide. *Love.*

Five more days until Christmas, Stevie, but we will do our best to keep the holiday spirit going all year.

Lesson #24: Be Grateful

Make everyday be like Christmas! By this, Daddy does not mean the presents, but the excitement and joy this holiday brings. Everyday we wake up is another gift given to us.

Since you were born, Daddy's thoughts oftentimes shift into panic mode when he thinks of all the things that could go wrong. You are so small and fragile which make the "what ifs" spin greater and stronger in his head. When Daddy's mind does go there, he now tunes the frequency to this lesson instead. Daddy is grateful for all the things he has and also grateful for all of the desired things that are not here yet because he is excited they are coming.

Every new day is a blessing to be cherished and loved. Make everyday count. Be grateful that life is so amazingly beautiful and full of joy. Seek these things out of life daily so everyday can be just like Christmas.

Look at that - Stevie's sleeping. Daddy cannot wait until you wake up again.

What an amazing first Christmas we had, Stevie. On Christmas Eve we took you to a beautiful candlelight service, and on Christmas Day all three of us were baptized. It was a very special day for your Mommy and Daddy. Today's lesson is a very touchy subject with some people so the only way Daddy can guide you is to be honest with how he feels.

Lesson #25: Believe In Whatever Brings You Love, Happiness And Peace

You did not have a choice in the baptism, but as you get older you will learn there are many ways to worship, pray and believe. You will learn there are many forms of spirituality and religion. There are also people who are not inclined to any religious beliefs. With this subject, there is no absolute right or wrong.

Eleven years ago, while Daddy was blacked out from drinking, he drove his car through two cement barricades. When he realized what happened, he asked God out of pure desperation to make Daddy never want to drink again. Eleven years later, he still does not want to drink.

The night Daddy found God, he also found peace. This is the path that works for him, but it does not mean it will be your path. To this day, Daddy still sees the beauty and simplicity in Taoism. As a scuba diver, he sees the beliefs of Darwin on a daily basis. Just because Daddy believes in God does not mean he is closed off from other forms of spirituality. Your Mommy has always been a believer in God and that has worked for her.

As you get older and you go through trying times, find whatever gives you love, happiness and peace. When you do find your path and believe wholeheartedly in that truth, then you should never feel the need to defend your viewpoint. When you can do this then you have found *your* love, happiness and peace.

Stevie, you were a bit fussy last night. You had your Mommy up all night. Maybe you are sensing something is about to change.

Lesson #26: Make Responsible Decisions Even When It Hurts

Mommy is going back to work. She has showered you with love from the time she knew you were in her belly. She was patient and waited for Daddy to catch up with her emotionally. He was not really there during the pregnancy. He was not a bad husband; he just could not fully grasp what was happening. Daddy is sorry for that, Natalie and Stevie.

Maternity leave is ending for Mommy and she is returning to her job. Sometimes, in order for families to be comfortable financially, the Mommy needs to go back to work. This was a truly gut wrenching decision for us to make. There were many heated discussions about this topic and it was very painful for Mommy when we came to this conclusion. But, we want to provide you with the best of everything. We want to travel and show you the world. In order to do this, we had to make this very difficult decision.

Again, Daddy thought he understood what Mommy was going to go through. Again, he was mistaken. Just because he went back to work right away did not mean he knew what she was experiencing. Just like when you were in her belly, Daddy misunderstood the gravity of the situation. Daddy can only grasp the magnitude now because he is so in love with you, Stevie.

Whenever you have to make a responsible decision, weigh the pros and cons. Do not be hasty. Even when that decision might hurt you, know that it is the right decision. Your Mommy sacrifices so much for you without a blink of an eye. When you are older and understand this lesson, wrap your arms around her and say "thank you!"

Well Stevie, a new year! Last New Year, Daddy was flipping out about this strange creature growing in Mommy's belly that was going to turn his life upside down and take all of his money. There is nothing poetic or deep about that statement, just the selfish truth. This new year, Daddy is the happiest and most complete he have ever been. Life does not have as many questions, and it should, right? There is not as much looking towards the future as there is living in now.

Lesson # 27: Deal With Life As It Comes So You Do Not Have To Clean Up The Messes Later

Things are going to happen in life which will make you uncomfortable or hurt you. There are going to be times where it is easier to ignore an unpleasant incident or pretend not to be bothered by it. If you let these situations pass and do not deal with them immediately, you have got a problem. This is not easy, Stevie. Daddy does not do a good job of expressing how he is feeling when he is hurt. He holds it in and becomes resentful. It is a quality that he is working to shift everyday. Once you are able to deal with life as it comes, then you can solve problems a lot quicker. You will have more time to live in today, than worry about yesterday, or what will come tomorrow. In order for you to believe in this lesson, then Daddy needs to keep working on it himself. He is so happy that he gets to see this new year through your eyes. Daddy is so happy that he has learned the most valuable lesson from you which is that he must live in today.

Mommy has been very strong, and in some ways stronger than Daddy. Two days ago, we left you with a babysitter for the first time. The night before, Daddy was sick with worry and the day we had to leave you, he made himself even sicker. We found two amazing babysitters who will take very good care of you, yet all of Daddy's thoughts were so negative.

Lesson #28: Keeping Eeyore Under Control Can And Will Make A World Of Difference

Your life will have some contrast, Stevie. Relationships are going to have bumps. Work will be difficult at times. People will not like you for no reason in particular. Sometimes, life can throw curve balls.

Daddy cannot wait for you to meet Winnie the Pooh and his friends. One of Winnie's friends is Eeyore. He is a really cute donkey, but all of his thoughts are so negative. Everything that Eeyore thinks and says is all doom and gloom. Poor Eeyore is trapped in a world that is always dark. For a long time Daddy was a lot like Eeyore. Daddy did not show this to the world, but inside everything was so sad and lonely. All of Daddy's thoughts were dismal and depressing. It has taken years to shed Daddy's inner Eeyore and the scary part is how easy it is to slip back and visit with him.

Daddy has not visited this old friend for a while, but the thought of something happening to you, he immediately went back to that dark place. Daddy still has some work to do, and thanks to Mommy, he was able to see that his pessimism had no value.

Daddy is not saying that all your thoughts will and should be positive. He wants you to be able to recognize when your fears or negativity are taking control of your life. It will happen, and it will not mean you are weak or bad, but that it is a feeling in a moment of time which will pass. We all have a little Eeyore in us which allows us to see that things are not always perfect. Eeyore is a friend that sometimes needs a little extra babysitting.

Lesson #29: Surround Yourself With People You Love And Who Love You Back

Love is such an amazing emotion. Love can make you laugh or cry, be happy or sad. Love can make you do things you never thought you would do. Love will bring closeness with others, which is intoxicating. Love will make you want to cuddle up on a cold snowy day, order pizza, turn off the TV, and talk the time away. Love will keep you up at night trying to figure out a way to make the day last a bit longer. Love makes you jump out of bed in the morning because you are so excited to get the day going. Love is always amazing, even when times may be tough. Yes love hurts sometimes, but once you work through it, you will see that you were better for having it in your experience.

Love can also be very complex. There are many different sides and shades of love and Daddy's inner Eeyore wants to warn you about and try to protect you from. We have years to sit and talk about love and there will be many life lessons on the topic, but today we are focusing on what love encompasses. Love is the thing you strive for in all that you do. Hopefully when you look in the mirror, what you see looking back is a whole lot of love. If you ever want to know what love looks like because you are having a difficult time finding it, take a moment and look directly in Mommy or Daddy's eyes. Daddy promises, you will always find love there.

Mommy stumped Daddy with a question today. She asked Daddy how he was going to explain the scars on his arms when you asked. He blew it off in the moment with what he thought was the true answer. Daddy responded to Mommy with, "the truth." After thinking about this for a few days, "the truth" is not a good enough answer.

Lesson #30: Always Be Proud Of Yourself

If you are not proud of who you are, then it is time to look in the mirror and see what is really going on. Daddy has been called a lot of things in his life. The one moniker he is most proud of and wants to be identified with is Daddy.

Daddy is so proud to be a parent, but with that comes amazing responsibility. The scars on his arms happened a long time ago. He was in a place where he really did not like himself. He made some mistakes back then, Stevie. Daddy was scared, confused, lonely, depressed, angry and selfish. He did not let loved ones help him, and he did not try to get help for himself. Daddy was not a happy person nor very proud of himself. He did a very selfish thing to himself twice and thank God he screwed up that as well.

For a couple of years Daddy hid those scars, and was very ashamed of them. It was not until he started to work on loving himself that he saw those scars differently. They are Daddy's battle scars. They are a daily reminder of how good his life has become. Now Daddy would not say he is proud of them, but he will tell you that he is proud of the man he has become. Those scars were a stepping stone to him becoming what he hoped to be - a good man and now more importantly, a very proud Daddy.

Stevie, you are the most important thing Daddy will ever be responsible for in this life. Daddy hopes that you will be proud to call him your Daddy.

Lesson #31: Do Not Let People Pop Your Balloons

Dream big, laugh hard, sing loud, travel everywhere.

Live life everyday not only like it is your last day, but also like it is your first.

See life with wide-eyed enthusiasm.

If life becomes mundane, change it.

Keep clear of people who drag you down.

Surround yourself with people who support the life you are living.

Be open to sharing what you learn with others. At the same time be open to letting go those who attempt to bring you down.

Love everyone, but trust in the love you have for yourself.

Live as you say you want to live.

Act as you want to act.

Be who you are and strive for the changes you want to see.

Always be yourself.

Make mistakes and learn from them.

Throw perfection out the window, and just do the best you can.

Love with all of you, and when you do get hurt, love yourself even harder.

This is your life and you choose how to live.

These are your balloons, Stevie. Only you should be allowed to pop these balloons when there are changes you want to make.

We had an emotional weekend, Stevie. It was two years ago today that your Grandpa Steve passed away. When we were sitting outside watching the whales on Sunday, it gave Daddy some time to reflect. Your Mommy told me a great story once about her and her Father, your Grandpa Steve. It was a beautiful story of two people who loved each very much, finally finding that father/daughter relationship they were missing. Today's lesson comes from that story and is not an easy lesson to learn. You may have a lot of trial and error with this one.

Lesson #32: You Cannot Change People, They Can Only Change Themselves

Now this can be a very confusing lesson for so many reasons. You are going to have people come into your life that you care about. Some of these people might hurt you. Sometimes people hurt others – at times on purpose and sometimes unintentionally.

Sometimes you will want to help people who are not ready to be helped.
Sometimes people will use your kindness for their own gain.
Sometimes you will have to let people go and other times you will have to fight for people.

Sometimes you will hurt the ones you love.
Sometimes people will let you go.

Daddy knows you may be confused, but simply put, life centers itself around relationships. Through all of these relationships, the hardest thing to learn is you cannot change people, nor should you want to change them. Only that person can change how they think and feel. Through constantly learning and working on yourself, you will see this is true. Through loving yourself, you will protect you. The most amazing thing is when a person changes who they are, because they see in you a living example of how they want to be.

A real relationship begins when you inspire someone so much that they have no choice but to look in the mirror and examine how they think and feel. Surround yourself with people that you inspire, but just as importantly, do the same for others. Your Mommy made Grandpa Steve look in the mirror, and an amazing relationship blossomed. You make Daddy look in the mirror everyday, and he keeps trying to figure out how to be the best version of himself. There is a lot in this lesson Stevie, but do not worry. Daddy promises, whenever you need help, we will be right here.

It is so amazing watching you grow, Stevie. You are developing your own little personality. So Daddy thinks you are ready to handle what may seem like an overwhelming challenge.

Lesson #33: Help Change The World!

Daddy knows you are probably thinking, "Daddy, I am only five months old. Can you at least wait until I am six months for this lesson?"

Stevie, the simple answer is no because you already are doing your part to change the world. This idea is not that crazy. And, it really is very easy to do. Here is an example - when Daddy takes you to the grocery store, strangers look at you and smile. Maybe some of them were having a bad day and hearing you laugh made them forget about things for a minute. Maybe your laugh put them in a better mood, and then they held the door open for someone who in return helped a child who dropped something and almost got yelled at by their mother. Wow Stevie, your little laugh just affected four people, all from a little giggle.

There are so many easy ways to help change the world. Smile as you pass people on the sidewalk. Hold a door open. Volunteer for a charity. Pay for someone's toll. Buy a stranger dinner and ask them to do the same one day. Call a friend you have not spoken to in a while. Be nice. Say please and thank you. Say I am sorry. You are only five months old and you have already showered people with smiles, laughs, and love. The best part is you do all of this stuff without even thinking about it because you are still connected to who you are at your core. See Stevie, changing the world really is not that hard. If you can do this at five months, then why not do it your entire life? Look at that smile! You are right Stevie, you know you just helped change the world for the better.

Lesson #34: Daddy Will Always Be Your Valentine

Daddy will always be your Valentine even when you get older and you start finding out all boys do not have cooties. Daddy will always be your Valentine even when you start da… daaay… daaayyttt…DATING! Daddy will always be your Valentine even when you go through that age where Daddy is all up in your business. Daddy will always be your Valentine even when you meet THE ONE. Whenever, however, whatever - he will always be there to put his arms around you and say, "Happy Valentines Day, Stevie. Daddy Loves You."

Now on a side note let us hold off on that whole dating thing until the Cubbies win the World Series. Deal?

Everyday you figure out a way to amaze Daddy. The speed at which you are learning new things blows his mind. He loves seeing the proud looks you give us when you do something you have never done before. The look of excitement when you discover something new fills his heart with joy.

Lesson #35: You Are Perfect Just the Way You Are

At this moment, there is nothing superficial in your energy. You are 100% honest with yourself because that is who you are. As we get older we tend to say things to make us look better. We may lie about experiences we have had. We may not be honest about our relationships. We may make up answers to questions we do not know so we do not look stupid.

If we are doing any of these things there is a problem. There is no reason to pretend to be something we are not. If a relationship is not healthy, work on nourishing it or end it. If we are missing experiences in our lives, then seek them out. If we do not know an answer to a question, find it, or simply say, "I don't know." If we are missing toys that others have and we want, then we should make a plan to work towards the goal of getting those toys.

When we look in the mirror, we should be happy with what we see.

Stevie, Daddy can honestly say that through the years he has been guilty of doing all of these negative things. He wanted people to believe his life was not the mess that he created. Daddy lived the rock star lifestyle and thrived on that energy. He wanted so badly not to miss out on anything that was going on at any given moment and wanted to be anywhere and everywhere. He created this persona because he was missing the key person in the equation – HIMSELF. Daddy had not found himself yet so he was looking outside of himself. This persona became who Daddy was for awhile.

His ego wanted other people to want to be envious of his crazy lifestyle. But that persona also got him into trouble because there was no balance. It was all go, go, go with no inner meditation.

Today, Daddy can look in the mirror and see himself. Today, he can look at you and see your perfection. As you get older and the pressures increase and you learn what jealousy, doubt and insecurity are - you are not alone. Daddy has two big shoulders that are always there for you to put your head on. Do not ever be too proud to ask for help if you are questioning yourself. Daddy's been down that road a few times and is here for you. Just remember you are perfect, Stevie, just the way you are.

Well Stevie, today's lesson is a sad one for Daddy. He has been holding this one from you because it is just not fair.

Lesson #36: Daddy Is Very Sorry

You have something growing in you that Daddy cannot stop. Even moving to Hawaii and being born in paradise cannot stop what is happening. Daddy's Grandpa had this Thing. Your Grandpa (Daddy's Daddy) gave this Thing to me. Your Mommy got this Thing from her Great Grandfather. Daddy hoped to protect you but he is afraid it is already too late. Stevie, it is an addiction like no other. At the beginning it is beautiful, hopeful, awe-inspiring, and exciting. By the end all you are left with is ugliness, disappointment, devastation and tears. There are people out there, even though they are just as miserable as we are, who will taunt us and engage in meaningless arguments because of this Thing. There is no cure. There is only pain and suffering. Daddy is so, so sorry, Stevie. You are a Cubs fan, and even though you do not know it now, Daddy knows it. He will do all he can to help you with this suffering. We will root hard, support and believe. We will cry, A LOT, but we will beat this Thing. One day we will go to Wrigley Field and you will be moved and inspired but not by the smell of beer, farts, drunks, or people partying and not caring about the game. You will see one of the last original stadiums and all of the great history of an amazing sport. You will hear a low hum in your ears that sounds a bit like "Go Cubs Go, Hey Chicago What Do You Say, The Cubs Are Gonna Win Today!" They will not have won, but that is just the way it usually is. You will learn four words which you will say over and over again: "Wait Till Next Year!!" This Thing is called Cubbie Blue. Take it for what it is, Stevie. Love it and hate it and, GO CUBBIES!

Lesson #37: There Are Times You Just Have To Let Go

This can be a hard lesson, Stevie. It can be very difficult when you feel like you do not have control of a situation. There will be many times where you will take charge of a situation. Sometimes, the results will be good, but there will also be times when things might not work out the way you wanted. But, you can take responsibility and handle the issue.

The tough moments are the ones where you think you have no control. That is when you just have to trust, believe in yourself and let go of the matter in question. Visualize what you want in the situation and then feel what it is like to be in the midst of the wanted outcome. Step back, take a deep breath, relax, and you will find the solution. Become the resolution. Stevie, sometimes you will swim upstream against the current and you will have lost your direction. Daddy is here to tell you that your internal compass will always work. You just have to let go of the problem, and know that the answer is always within reach inside of you.

Today's lesson is one of those reality checks we have to do from time to time.

Lesson #38: Every Now And Then We Need To Shut Our Mouths and Listen

We do not like to hear we are not doing enough. We do not like others to tell us we are doing something wrong. We do not like to be judged, criticized, questioned, blamed or second-guessed. When it comes to our behavior, feelings, ideas, or way of life we think we know what is best for us. Now add love to the mix and everything just got a lot bigger!

When we truly love someone, we feel that everything we are doing is being done out of love. That part is true. When we love, we usually treat that person with the utmost respect. The people in our lives who we love usually get to see us at our very best. They get to see our strengths, passions and desires. But, they also see our weaknesses, dislikes, and our fears. People who love each other love the good and get through the bad together.

Here is the heart of the lesson, Stevie. If the same problem keeps arising which causes the same arguments in different relationships, then it is time for a gut check. You need to shut your mouth, leave your ego at the door, hang up the pride, go somewhere alone and be honest with yourself. Yep, there are times when this will have to be done. Once we dig deep, we can break old beliefs. We can change our way of thinking for the better. Love is beautiful, amazing, and exciting. Love can also be scary at times. We live and we learn through love. It is a good thing when someone loves you enough to tell you a positive change must be made. Stevie, Daddy dedicates this lesson to your Mommy. She loves Daddy enough to stand beside him and when it is necessary, makes him shut his mouth and listen.

Stevie, it has been one very stressful week. Actually the past few months have been hectic and several challenging situations have been present recently. Reflection and Mommy's guidance have brought Daddy to today's lesson.

Lesson #39: Get Your Butt Off That Pity Pot!

What is a pity pot, Stevie? It is a place that is so easy for Daddy to visit. Once stress sets in, if he does not check it really fast, you can find Daddy on his pity pot. It is where he sits so everyone can see him feeling sorry for himself. It is a place where Daddy feels so comfortable when he is feeling uncomfortable. It is a place where you can always find him when he does not want to let go. Sometimes we think that circumstances in life have all the control. But here is a secret Daddy learned - if you change your perspective on the subject, your viewpoint on that subject will shift.

Or sometimes you just have to say, "God grant me the serenity to accept the thing I cannot change." Guess what? It really is that simple. Then why does Daddy fight it so often and sit on his pity pot? Fear. It is scary when you think you do not have control of what is happening, and it is having a huge impact on your life. Individually, we all need the "courage to change the things we can," but most of all we need the "wisdom to know the difference." When Daddy does not let go of things he has no control of, then he is not working on bettering himself.

Daddy has worked very hard on himself over the years. When he lets fear put him back on his pity pot, then he is not looking at himself in the mirror. He is letting fear control his life. It is amazing how so many of these lessons coincide with each other. Be your own cheerleader, Stevie. Recognize when you are sitting on your pity pot. When you are, ask for help and work on yourself - but most of all LET GO. You only hurt yourself when you stop working on you. Shift your outlook on things. You always hold all the answers. If you ever find yourself on the pity pot, Stevie, just know it is okay to let go and use your two biggest cheerleaders. Mommy and Daddy will always be there for you with poms-poms and a baton.

Today is a very special day for Daddy. All of these lessons started to take shape eleven years ago today. It is also ironic that Daddy is forty years old and this is lesson #40. Without this decision, there would be no lessons coming from Daddy.

Lesson #40: Be Self Aware

The first thing you need to know about this lesson is that Daddy is an alcoholic. He does not know if he truly believes that alcoholism is hereditary, but wants to share this side of him with you so your aware. Daddy did not have his first drink until he was eighteen, and did not have his first drunk until twenty-one. In today's world, that is incredible. During Daddy's ten year drinking and drugging career, he more than made up for the late start.

Daddy used alcohol to not feel. He used alcohol to be someone he was not. Daddy hated who he was or was not, so he drank to the point of not feeling. He does believe that alcoholism is a disease. Daddy knew he was forming an addiction, and romanticized the addiction. He was proud of being a drunk that no one understood. Daddy hurt so many people as he was slowly killing himself. At the end, Daddy was almost completely alone. There were a few people that had not given up on him yet, but that is only because they had not been around it long enough. Long story short Stevie, Daddy crashed his car and should have died.

The police and medics could not explain how Daddy came through with very minor injuries. Daddy was defeated and back then, he was only a Believer when he needed something. When he came back into consciousness, he asked God to take away the desire to drink. Eleven years later, Daddy still has not desired another drink.

One day, when you are older, Daddy will tell you the whole story in detail. He will tell you this not to stop you from drinking or experimenting, but so you can be aware. He hopes you can go out and have drinks and enjoy the social aspects of drinking and the fun that it can bring while still being responsible. However, if you do run into trouble, Daddy wants you to know you can always come to him.

Daddy is a man who is still growing and learning. Drinking was something he did but it will not define who he is. Daddy loves who he is more every day. He is blessed to have such an amazing woman who loves him. Daddy is blessed to have a daughter whom he loves more than he ever knew was possible. Daddy has a family. Today and everyday, Daddy thanks his higher power, because without You none of this would be possible.

Happy Easter, Stevie! Between learning to clap and crawling for the first time, Mommy and Daddy could not take our eyes off you. We were afraid we would miss something new.

Lesson #41: Just When You Think You Have It All Figured Out, You Realize You Do Not

Daddy thought he had it figured out so many times before. Daddy was going to be a pro baseball player, but then hurt his shoulder. Daddy was going to be a movie star, but so were a million others. Daddy was going buy a house, pay it off, have a growing savings account, and then the housing market went down the toilet. He was going to travel the world to teach scuba diving, and then Mommy stole his heart. Mommy and Daddy were going to have a very difficult time having a baby, and eleven months later, HERE IS STEVIE!

Looking at this small list, not including ceasing drugs and alcohol, Daddy has had many rebirths. No matter how tight a grip you think you have, life is full of surprises. Things change, circumstances change, times change and…life happens. How you adapt to these changes Stevie, will define how you will treat your journey. Change may not always be good at first, but then you find the good within those circumstances. Change can be amazing and a breath of fresh air. Sometimes it makes you look in the mirror and changes your perspective for the better. You will think you have done the work, only to realize there is more work to be done.

Daddy had it all figured out before you got here Stevie, and in less than eight months you have taught him forty one new lessons which showed Daddy that he will never figure it all out. Life is full of surprises which is where you can find fun and joy. Change can be amazing and if you allow it in, change will show you that life is truly beautiful.

It is a big day today, Stevie! It is Mommy's birthday! It was so nice of you to get her a card that says just how much you love her. This morning, after letting Mommy sleep for eight whole hours, you wrapped your arms around her and gave her a big hug. It was like you knew it was her birthday.

Lesson #42: Show And Tell

Daddy's family had a hard time expressing emotion. Growing up, it would feel cold and lonely at times. Daddy knows that is mean to say, but it was true. We never said we loved each other, and you would never catch us hugging one another.

Even today if we even try to do any loving things for one another, there is a weird discomfort in the air. Daddy feels badly about this Stevie, and it ends with you, Mommy and Daddy.

If you care about someone, it is okay to hug them. It seems so strange that Daddy even has to write that, but he feels like he should explain himself. Show the ones you love that you love them. Hug each other, hold hands, put an arm around one another, and kiss each other hello and goodbye. These wonderful little gestures are what make us human. It is amazing how a squeeze on the shoulder is better than fifteen minutes of someone talking about how they know what you are going through.

Take it a step further and tell the ones you love, "I LOVE YOU!" It is so easy to say. Feel it, say it, and mean it, Stevie. Do not use these three words against someone. Do not withhold these words as a form of control. Do not say it to get what you want.

When you say "I love you," embody the words. Do not ever let the power of these three words lose their meaning.

Tell the people you love that you love them every chance you get. Love is a beautiful thing. In its true form it is as innocent as you are now. You will have lots of ups and downs when it comes to love, as we all do. Growing pains happen because we love. When love hurts, learn why it hurts. Love deeply because of your experiences. If you ever question love or what love is, look in Mommy or Daddy's eyes. He promises you will see nothing but true love in its most innocent form. If you ever need to feel love, wrap your arms around Mommy or Daddy. You will receive a hug that does not require words. Daddy's promises he will never make you feel uncomfortable about showing your love. Daddy loves you, Stevie! Let us go get Mommy her birthday cake!

Your first tooth! Daddy thought he was ready for this development, but he was wrong. Mommy was so excited when she saw your tooth. Daddy, well Daddy, got really upset. You are becoming so independent. You do not want to be held as much. You are crawling and pulling yourself up anyway you can. When you fall, you are not always looking to us for reassurance. You are entertaining yourself. You are becoming this little person so fast. GRRRRRRR!

Well listen here Miss Stevie Kai, Lesson #43: You Will Always Be My Baby!

No matter how fast you learn how to walk, you will always be my baby. When you are ready to start feeding yourself, you will still be my baby. When you do not need diapers anymore (and please hurry up with this one), you will always be my baby. When you pick out your own clothes and dress yourself (this one is for you Mommy), you will always be my baby. When you take the bus to school, you will always be my baby. When you start dating (at age thirty seven), you will still be my baby. When you start your own life, you will always be my baby. Daddy is going to have a real hard time letting you become an adult but he promises that he will do everything he can to help you when you need guidance.

Daddy treasures all these wonderful experiences you are having and he adores everything new that you see with your wide-eyed stares. His heart explodes with love with every smile, laugh, look, noise, and hug you give him. No matter what is going on in your life, Daddy wants you to come to him. Let him share in your success, and be there for you in your disappointments. Daddy loves the little person you are becoming, but you will always be his baby.

Stevie, shhhhhhhh....we are going to let Mommy sleep in this morning. One day you will realize the best gift for Mommy is to let her sleep.

Lesson #44: You Have One Amazing Mommy

Stevie, from the day Mommy knew you were in her belly, you became her world. While Daddy was trying to wrap his brain around this whole thing and basically doing nothing, Mommy leaped over dumbfounded Daddy in a single bound, and started preparing for your arrival. Faster than clueless Daddy, Mommy took care of everything. More powerful than any man Daddy knows, Mommy put together a crib, a dresser, and a changing table. It was amazing, it was awesome, and it was Mommy!

She read books, researched on the computer, and asked thousands of questions. Daddy...well Daddy hung out with the crickets. All of a sudden a tornado came to Kailua-Kona and the aftermath left diapers, wipes, bottles, a breast pump, and everything a newborn baby could need. Daddy assisted with his usual charm, "Honey, do we really need this?"

A tidal wave hit next and the waves brought lots of beautiful clothes, for the soon to be best dressed baby in all of Hawaii. Finally there was the earthquake that turned our tiny, one bedroom condo into a cozy home for our new family. Mommy did all of this on her own. Thank God she needed a little something from him to make you (Mommy will talk to you about that in about thirty seven years) or Daddy could not take any credit.

On this Mother's Day, Daddy wants you to know that you have one amazing Mommy. She is his Superhero. She is your SuperMommy.

Lesson #45: There Is Nothing In Life Which You Cannot Accomplish

This lesson might seem a bit over the top, but it is true. Whatever you may be passionate about you can seek it, find it, learn about it, study it, do it, and live it. If there is something you want to know more about, there are thousands of resources to help you. If you want to travel to various parts of the world, there are many ways to get there.

Doors can be unlocked if you want them opened. Dreams are within reach if you seek after them. Do not let anyone tell you what you cannot be. Surround yourself with people who make you be a better person and share your zest for life. Open your eyes everyday and see all the miracles that happen right in front of your eyes. Big miracles are astounding, but the little ones are what make it so incredible to wake up every morning. Be the best you can be and your dreams will come true. Live your life by your rules and become who you want to become. If you want to be a professional baseball player or the President, then be the best Presidential Cubbie you can be. Live life, laugh at and with life, and most of all love life. Your journey is whatever you choose it to be and you can make it as incredible and amazing as you want!

Wow, what a week Stevie! You met your Grandpa for the first time and we had an amazing two days. Looking back over these lessons, Daddy realized that he told you how much he wanted you, Mommy and Daddy to be a close family. He has told you how his family is not very close. Well Stevie, Daddy realized that he had been doing you an injustice.

Lesson #46: Family Is So Very, Very Important

All Daddy has revealed to you is that his side of the family is not intimate and how he wants things to be different. After the visit with Grandpa and talking with Mommy, Daddy opened his eyes. He had to sit back and look at his role and take responsibility in the family situation. Is Daddy doing everything in his power to try and bring his family closer together? The very simple answer is no.

It was so amazing and beautiful to see Grandpa holding you, Stevie. It brought Daddy back to when he was a little boy and how much he loved Grandpa. When Daddy was a kid, Grandpa was his hero. Daddy is not sure when the disconnect happened in his family, but that really does not matter. What matters is what Daddy does now to try and get the family connected again. He cannot say "I want to be a close family," and then do nothing. Your Grandpa has many amazing qualities about him, and Daddy is so excited for you to learn what they are.

We all have things that we need to work on. The problem is we usually spend so much of our time trying to fix others, when we should be spending that time looking inward. Look at qualities in other people that make them amazing and love them for those traits. Help others only if they ask. Most of all let the ones you love sort things out for themselves. When it comes right down to it, we are the only ones who can find our own balance and alignment. And once we do, we can take the steps hopefully needed to get to a desired result.

Wow, Stevie, what an amazing birthday Daddy had today! He received birthday wishes from all over the world. There was an overwhelming feeling of being blessed in the air and an abundance of gratitude to know so many amazing people all over this HUGE planet. This was also his first birthday as a Daddy and what a stellar day you and Mommy gave him!

Lesson #47: Use Your Birthday To Reflect On Your Blessings

This birthday was very special because of you, Stevie. Daddy has the two best presents in the world: a best friend whom he married and an unconditional love that he gives to and receives from you. The third present was unexpected because it happened as Daddy started to examine his life to date.

As he reflected on many moments over the years, he realized there were additional things he wanted to work on to continue to evolve. Daddy talks a lot about wanting to live in the present moment and letting life unfold organically but then not always adhering to these mantras. It seems whenever Daddy gets all out of whack it is because he is pushing against life.

Daddy made the decision to try to be conscious and present in the moment. The past is just that -- the past tense. The future has not arrived yet and will never get here if we are always looking for it. The work done in the past is what should allow Daddy to stay in the present. This process has made him look in the mirror (there it is again, Lesson #1) and has brought on so many different emotions. One of them came flooding out on his birthday -- he is so blessed. Your Mommy and you complete a circle of family and friends from all over the world that have touched Daddy's life in so many remarkable ways that words cannot describe his appreciation. Daddy is looking in the mirror and taking the necessary steps to be a better father, husband, and friend. By doing this work it makes it so easy to receive the love given, but more importantly, give the love back. Everyday you should remind yourself how blessed you truly are, but what better day than your birthday is there to reflect on how loved you are by others.

Thank you, Stevie, for making Daddy's first Father's Day so amazing. You came to work with him, and Mommy and Daddy went on a dive together! Mommy saw her very first tiger shark, and even lived to tell about it.

Lesson #48: There Are Things That Make You Feel Uneasy At First But Then You Fall In Love With Them

Mommy would probably never have gone scuba diving if it were not for Daddy. She was very scared and uncertain about the whole thing. Mommy was also terrified of sharks so Daddy did not push her to dive, but she saw how much he loved the ocean and decided to give it a try. When Mommy saw her first shark she was very afraid, but then she realized that they are beautiful and not out to eat people so she grew to love sharks as well. Initially, Mommy created a lot of this fear in her head. She decided to change the way she saw and thought about sharks, was able to overcome her fear, and now loves to scuba dive.

Daddy had a different fear. He was very scared to be a Daddy. Would he be a good Daddy? How could he afford a baby? How would he know what to do? How would he find the time to be a Daddy? Could he really love a baby, and give up the way he lived his life? Wow, so many questions that he let overcome all of his thoughts.

Today Daddy looks at all those questions and they do not resonate anymore. When he laid eyes on you for the first time, there was a shift; a shift in thinking, feeling, seeing, and loving. Any questions he obsessed over were gone. Now the only question Daddy asks is if could he love this little package any more. Everyday, he finds out that answer is YES. Daddy loves you more today than he did yesterday, and he bets that will be the same tomorrow. When things get uneasy in life, Stevie, it is not always a struggle, but a way to challenge yourself and see what is behind the lesson. As you evolve into who you are, learn from these challenges. Maybe you will end up loving the challenge that initially made you feel uneasy.

Stevie, you blew Daddy away on the Fourth of July as you stared up into the sky and were amazed by the beautiful fireworks. You sat like a little adult as you received your first haircut. YOU ARE TAKING YOUR FIRST STEPS! You have put up with Mommy and Daddy passing you around to different people. You have made so many people laugh and smile with your babbling and emerging personality. You have turned into this incredible force of nature known as "Tornado Stevie" and nothing stays in place in the midst of your storm.

Lesson #49: Life Moves Really Fast And Change Is Inevitable

Life moves very fast, Stevie. Change is definitely inevitable. The key to this is how you handle what life throws at you and sometimes Daddy needs help in this area. You are changing everyday and handling it so well. Daddy needs to learn this lesson from you. You just go with it. Life happens and you just flow with its current. Many people would say, "she's just a baby, she doesn't know any better." That is one of the incredible things about you. You innately know to just go with it.

Watching you grow so fast is awesome. Every time you stop doing one amazing thing, you start a new thing that is just as incredible. You do not give Daddy time to question the changes. It is either he accepts the change and moves on, or fights the change. If Daddy fights the change, he runs the risk of completely missing out on all the awesomeness which is you in that moment. Change is good. Life is fast and beautiful. As long as Daddy has his two ladies, it will be one incredible roller coaster ride.

Daddy has not been looking forward to today because he has to leave you for four days to attend a seminar. He is only going to be away from you and Mommy for a few days, but this is extremely hard. You just got over your first illness where you had a fever for five days. You were such a strong girl during this time, and even though you were not feeling your best, you still kept a smile on your face a lot of the time. Daddy is going to take that lesson of resilience with him.

Lesson #50: You Are Only As Good To Others As You Are To Yourself

It may sound selfish, Stevie, but you are number one. If you are not healthy than how can you assist others? Your mental, emotional, and physical being are all your responsibility. Right now Mommy and Daddy take care of everything you need, but there will come a time when this responsibility will become solely yours. That is not to say we will not be there for you - you will never get rid of us that way. What Daddy means by this is that you will take charge of your own life. Taking care of yourself will be a responsibility that will be exciting. Daddy knows in his heart that when he comes back he will be much better mentally, emotionally, physically, and most of all spiritually. This makes it a bit easier to leave you both for a few days.

Be in tune with you, Stevie. When something does not seem right it is usually because something is off. Emotional, mental, physical, and spiritual issues are only problems if you choose to ignore them when they arise. When there is something stopping you from being the best you, deal with it to better yourself. When you do not deal with your problems, there is only so much you can sweep under the rug before you notice a lumpy carpet. It is Daddy's intention to return from this seminar stronger and continue to evolve as a father, a husband and a person.

Today's lesson is going to be hard to understand until you get a bit older. Right now you get to eat what Mommy and Daddy give you. We pick out the outfits you wear, the toys you have, and your play dates. Your choices are plenty, but you do not have very much say so. As you get older and start making these choices for yourself, you will sometimes come to a fork in the road. One way might lead down an easy path, and another might lead to a great unknown. One road might require a lot of work for an incredible payoff, and another might require even harder work for a greater reward. It is these choices and roads you will travel that will define all you give and receive out of life and love.

Lesson #51: Never Settle

Today is Mommy and Daddy's four year anniversary. The greatest gift Daddy received before you came along was meeting, falling in love, and marrying your Mommy. He kissed a lot of frogs before he met Mommy. Or maybe he should say a lot of frogs kissed him before he met Mommy. No, Stevie, you cannot kiss a frog yet.

Daddy took a lot of different roads in his life and some of them were bumpy. There were many times he thought about going back on the road he had been on previously even though it did not bring happiness. There was comfort in that familiarity. We do that, Stevie. We stay on certain roads even though we do not grow. We stay because we are comfortable. We stay because we know the outcome. We stay because there are no questions and because we fear change. Even if we know there is a better road, a lot of times fear will cause us to not investigate a new pathway. So Daddy stayed on this bumpy road and dealt with all the pot holes, slick spots, and fog. One day, he swerved a little to the left, and the road improved and became much easier to navigate. It was filled with sunlight. At the end of that road he saw Mommy. She was walking down the street and Daddy lost his breath. He had to meet this beautiful woman. We locked eyes, and Mommy said, "if you thought the road you were just on was tough, wait till we get on this new road." Guess what? Mommy was right. This road is very tough at times, but also so amazingly beautiful. The best part is Mommy and Daddy drive down this road together. In life you do not ever have to settle, Stevie. Sometimes good things come very easily. Sometimes you might have to work a bit for something better. Other times you may have to work until you cannot work anymore, and those times words will not describe the joy in your heart. When it comes to LOVE Stevie, do not ever allow yourself to settle.

HAPPY FIRST BIRTHDAY, STEVIE KAI! One year ago you made your appearance into this world. You came out not breathing, and freaked out your already freaked out Daddy. Finally, you started breathing on your own and from that moment on you have owned Daddy's heart. You have taught him so many lessons on how to LIVE. You have taught him the true meaning of LOVE. Watching you learn new things has made him LAUGH like he has never laughed before.

Lesson #52: LIVE, LOVE, LAUGH

We are celebrating your first birthday with a big party. We are going to rejoice being alive. Daddy is sure there is going to be a whole lot of laughing, especially with your imitation of a drunken sailor as you walk. Most of all he is sure you are going to be surrounded by love. Seek love and laughter in all things and before you know it, your life will be exactly where you want it to be.

Live everyday giving love and laughter. Life is going to happen so choose how you are going to live it. There will be bad days, moments, and times. Such is life. Yet, it is up to you to choose how to look at any of these days, moments, and times.

Take moments and add love and some laughter. Do not limit your expectations. Always assume the best. Life will unfold and you should take in all the good and learn from all of the bumps. Surround yourself with love and laughter. You will become contagious and people will be drawn to celebrate life with you.

Happy Birthday, Stevie. Thank you for helping Daddy LIVE LIFE with LOVE and LAUGHTER.

It has been a hectic couple of months. First we opened up a new business. Then it was your birthday. We took you to meet your family on the mainland. We moved into our new house. Then we turned this house into a home. Now it is time to try and get back to normal. All of these events were very exciting, but also caused a bit of stress.

Lesson #53: Life Is Less Stressful When You Have Someone You Love Standing Next To You

Daddy is sure you have witnessed Mommy and him bickering quite a bit over the last few months. There have been times where you were probably a bit confused by the stress and tension that was surrounding us. Through all of this you figured out a way to put smiles on our faces. Daddy is so happy to have Mommy here to help battle the storms. When life is throwing all it has at you, there is nothing more incredible than to be able to have someone you love have your back. Mommy and Daddy could not be where we are today without each other. Through all the bad times, arguments and miscommunications, we always had each others hands to hold as we fell asleep. Today we have a beautiful daughter, a place to call home, a love that has been through so much and still shines brightly, and most of all a sense of peace. Our love will carry us, always. "Everything's gonna be alright," Stevie, just like your favorite Bob Marley song says.

Lesson #54: No Matter What Life Is Throwing At You, There Will Always Be A Reason To Be Thankful

Life is amazing, exciting, adventurous, beautiful, innocent, loving, and so many other wonderful things. But, you will have bad days. Days might go by where you feel a little off. There will be days where you have had enough and want to sneak under the covers. These are the days where you just have to look inside. Sometimes you may have to look deep inside to find something to be thankful about in that moment. Daddy promises there will always be something to be grateful for in your life. Sometimes bad days show up because of how we deal with a certain situation. When you are stuck in an uncomfortable place, try looking at that place differently. When we are in a circumstance we do not like, look at the circumstance with new eyes. Bad days can usually be turned around by deciding you want to make them better. There will be challenges that will shake your world up so badly, you may want to get back to basics and simplify the contrast so you can see your way out. The thing is Stevie, there is always a way out. What makes life so ridiculously awesome is the simple fact that everyday you will see thousands of things to be thankful for and all you need to do is look. Live, Love, Laugh and life will usually take care of itself and shower you with gifts.

Lesson #55: Always Look For The Light

There are things that will happen that might make you question your beliefs. There might be moments that will shock you to the core of disbelief. There will be events that might waiver your faith in this world. Daddy cannot answer why sad things happen sometimes. Daddy's theory is that without the melancholy, how would anyone know the true meaning of joy?

No matter how depressing something may seem, there is always a better place. Look at the world from a place of love, not judgment. When you look for the light, you will always find it in any situation. There are moments when Daddy looks at world events and sees darkness. Daddy wants to put you in a bubble and surround you with all that is good but that is not a way to live.

You have a magic power, Stevie. You can make anybody smile. You ooze love in every direction. You see the world as a big playground full of amazing and wonderful things. You can take a box and play for hours. You can take an empty bag and fill it with all the wonders of your world. As you get older remember these places. Remember that life is innocent and beautiful. Remember that people do want to smile and laugh. Remember that love is all around you and sometimes it is easy to see, and sometimes you will see it with a bit of effort. Remember that you are full of an endless supply of love. What does Daddy always say to you, Stevie? Live, Love, and Laugh. A heavy dose of that everyday will help you out on those difficult days. It will make you see the light. It also reminds Daddy to look for the light, even when he sees darkness.

This lesson is dedicated to Daddy's Grandpa, who passed away this morning. It is a blessing to know that Stevie shared some of her love with you.

Lesson #56: Make Time To Visit With The Ones You Love

It is ridiculous how busy we make ourselves. We work too much. We worry too much. We waste too much time worrying and working. We say we are going to call, write, visit, Skype, come over, go out, meet up… the list is endless and we usually do not have time for anything. During the holidays that seems to change a little and we seem to find the time. The funny thing is when we do force ourselves to make the time, we usually have the best time! Is that not ridiculous?! Find the balance, Stevie. Talk with your Grandparents. Visit with your best friend. Go on holiday with the girls. Have dinner with Mommy and Daddy. Skype with people who live far away. Share your precious time with the people you care about and love. It is simply the best advice Daddy can give you.

Happy New Year, Stevie! This last year was incredible. How much you have changed in one year is unbelievable! Daddy changed a lot too. He allowed himself to grow and has you to thank for this metamorphosis. When you get older, you are going to hear about New Year's resolutions. New Year's has become a time for people to try something different, change who they are, or think differently. It is a wonderful thing when you look inside, see a change that needs to be made, and transform.

Lesson #57: If Something Is Not Right In Your World, CHANGE IT

Why wait until New Year's? Change can be hard, it may take a while and it may be scary. Regardless, if you are not feeling right about something, change it. Why wait? Waiting means you are allowing yourself to be stuck, and what good does that do you? Most of the time there is a really simple way to change. Change the way you think about the situation. Once you can do this, now you can take action. A lot of times, just doing this will even resolve the situation. There is no doubt that change will be very difficult at times. These are the times where it is so critical that you allow change. Daddy has had to change many times in his life. He has had to knock down many walls. He had to look into very scary rooms. Through all of those times Daddy has changed, it has always been for the better. We are constantly evolving. This is how we grow. This is how we become so amazing. This is how we live. This is how we love. By watching how quickly you change, Stevie, you have taught Daddy just how quickly we can shift our lives if we put our mind to it and be present in the moment. Daddy's New Year's resolution is simple this year. He is going to be the best Daddy. When he runs into any walls, you have already taught him how to blow them up. BOOM!

Lesson #58: People Can And Do Change

This can be a tough lesson because there are times when change may cause the end of a relationship. There are times when two people may grow apart and go their separate ways. There are times when two people may grow in different directions. There are times when two people need to leave one another. These times can be hard. You will have relationships that will end, many friendships that will fade, and many events that will send you in different directions. These times may cause heartache, loneliness, confusion, anger and all sorts of discomfort. Through these times it is critical to feel all that you are feeling. It is important to see the truth. It is vital to learn and grow from these times.

Look in the mirror, Stevie, and take these difficult times and turn them into a positive. Just as you go through life and change and grow, so will everybody you know and love. One of the most amazing and beautiful things you will ever see is when someone you know realizes that with change they will get more out of life. When someone you love embraces, accepts, and loves the change they are going through, they embrace, accept, and love themselves. It is amazing to watch a person who is overweight lose the pounds and gain self confidence. It is amazing to hear an alcoholic admit they have a problem and work towards sobriety. It is amazing to see a victim stand up for themselves. It is amazing to see a person turn a negative into a positive. That is the beauty of life.

You cannot change people, but you can be there for them. You can be an ear to listen, a shoulder to rest on, a back to lean on, and arms to wrap around them and hug tight. People can and do change. It almost always is for the best, but when it is not, love them anyway.

Daddy loves all the changes you have brought into his world.

It is funny how life works almost all of the time. Daddy thought he had done a decent job with these last two lessons on change, and was ready to move on. This is a hard one, Stevie, but he feels it covers a little piece of almost every lesson we have talked about so far.

Lesson #59: Saying Goodbye Can Be Hard

Your Grandma passed away last night, Stevie. This was not unexpected, but it still happened a lot faster than Daddy expected. In the last year, since you started babbling and talking away, we would have our afternoon date on the phone

31

with Grandma. During these dates, Daddy would hear the love in her voice every time you said something. He knows you enjoyed these times as well. You would smile ear to ear when you heard Grandma say hello to you.

Saying goodbye to someone we love is so hard. It seems unfair that we should even have to endure such pain. The thing is we do not really have to say goodbye. Daddy will tell you all about your Grandma. He will do the best he can, so you feel like you knew her. He can tell you that Grandma had a difficult second half of her life. This is why change is so important. This is why growing as a person is so important. This is why looking in the mirror is so important. Your Grandma is now at peace. The demons that she battled are gone now.

The one thing that you will come to know is Grandma gave love freely. She would drop anything in a second if her kids needed anything. If one of Grandma's children was in trouble, she was there to help with the problem and shower them with love. As you get older, Stevie, we will talk, laugh, and cry as Daddy shares stories about Grandma with you. We will not have our phone dates anymore, but you bet we will still be talking to Grandma every day.

The past two weeks have been a lesson in growth. Grandma's passing is something Daddy would probably have never been ready for because how do you prepare yourself for the passing of a parent? Emotions of anger, despair, sadness, hate, loneliness, bitterness, shock and numbness all come in waves. Sometimes the waves are powerful and other times they are very subtle and unassuming. Mourning is a process where there are no instructions. There is no timetable. There is no right or wrong. Sometimes Daddy feels guilty because he does not feel emotions so strongly. And then it hits him hard like tidal wave crashing into his head.

Lesson #60: Make Good On Any Regrets You Have

If you have any regrets, and you do not take care of them, they will almost always figure out a way to come back to haunt you. If Grandma would have passed away, say three years ago, Daddy may have been going through an entirely different mourning process.

Daddy and Grandma had a very strenuous relationship through the years. For a long time, he did nothing about the strained bond except wish he had a better relationship with Grandma. Wishing and acting are two different things. When you wish, things MAY get better. When you act, things WILL get better. A bad situation will stay that way, if you do not change that situation. There is that word CHANGE again.

Daddy worked really hard on the connection with Grandma. The first thing he did was change how he looked at the situation. He stopped trying to change who Grandma was and instead loved her for who she was. Once he changed his thinking, the process of working on the relationship became easy. Daddy and Grandma worked on their bond and in the end had a mutual love for one another. Was it a fairy tale relationship? No, but it was a beautiful relationship.

The reason why Daddy was not feeling awful emotions as he was mourning was because all he feels for Grandma is love. Yes, he is sad and misses talking with Grandma very much. Yes, it brings a tear to his eyes when he thinks about you not truly knowing her. Yet in the end Daddy knows that he was blessed to have a relationship with Grandma that was filled with spice and smothered in love.

Lesson #61: Never Miss An Opportunity To Tell Someone How Much You Love Them

It feels good to love. It feels amazing to be in love. When you love someone, tell them every chance you get that you love them. Daddy thinks he tells you a hundred times a day that he loves you, and some days even more. That does not mean you should walk around all day saying, "I love you, I love you, I love you." That may get a tad annoying after a while. There is an infinite number of ways to tell someone you love them: a hug, a smile, a look, a note, a gift, running their errand. The list goes on and on. Do not ever be ashamed or feel the need to hide your feelings for the people you care about in your life. If you are ever doing that Stevie, it should tell you there is something wrong. If that is ever happening, change it! You will usually find that these are the times that the love you are seeking is not being reciprocated or that you need to let the person go.

Love is bigger than us! You can try to understand all there is about love, and you will still never understand it completely. The best way to do it is with a KISS. Keep it simple, Stevie! Love being in Love. Love others. Share Love. Accept Love. Feel Love. Express Love. Seek Love. Most of all... Love Yourself.

Stevie, you keep looking in the other bedroom to see if Grandpa is in there. He will be back for another visit soon. You really took a loving to Grandpa on this last visit. Daddy will fill you in on a little secret, Grandpa did too. It was like watching Daddy's childhood all over again, except this time it was through your eyes, Stevie. Daddy also came to a realization on this last visit with Grandpa.

Lesson #62: It Is Not About How We Love

We cannot make someone love us the way we want to be loved because they can only love us the way they know how to love. Confused? Here is an example of what Daddy is trying to say. Daddy loves chocolate. Mommy does not love chocolate. It would be silly if he expected Mommy to love chocolate in order for Daddy to know that she loved him.

Every person you will meet in your lifetime has been brought up in a different way than you. What makes us all so amazing is how different we all are. We all have learned who to love, when to love, what to love, where to love, how to love, and why to love...differently. We all express, show, teach, give, and feel love differently. We all love differently. That is not an odd statement if you think about how love is so amazing and beautiful, and in the same breath so hard and confusing at times.

What got Daddy thinking about this was watching Grandpa play with you, Stevie. Daddy saw Grandpa as he remembered him as a child. Grandpa was an amazing Father and now is an even more amazing Grandparent. Daddy will take what he learned about love from Grandpa and shower you with it every day. Maybe it will be with a story before bed, or by being the biggest fan at your games, or by lending you an arm to lift you up when you fall. Daddy thinks he will be pretty good at these things because he learned from a great teacher. We all love differently, Stevie, and that is what makes life so extraordinary and rarely ever boring.

It has been so busy! There have been so many guests coming to visit us, Stevie. You have been having so much fun and have been such a great hostess. Daddy loves the way you captivate everybody you come into contact with all the time. You take life and turn it into one big playground. We have been talking so much lately about love, so let us continue with that, plus throw in a dash of laughter, and a sprinkle of life.

Lesson #63: Throw Seriousness Out Of The Window Every Chance You Get

Daddy is not saying to never be serious. There will be many times in your life where you will have to make serious decisions. There will be many times in your life where you will have to do some serious thinking. There will also be many times in your life where you will have to seriously look in the mirror. "Daddy, why so serious? Didn't you just say throw seriousness out of the window every chance you get?"

As an adult, there seems to be so much seriousness. There are so many responsibilities, bills to pay, work to go to, errands to run, messes to clean up, problems to fix…blah, blah, blah. The list is endless. So as adults, what is the first thing we do? We throw fun out of the window every chance we get!

"Fun? I don't have no time for that!"
"Get together? Sorry, busy!"
"Enjoy life? With what time?"

These are all excuses and Daddy calls shenanigans. Stop the MADNESS! Life is too amazing to live this way. All of this MADNESS is going to be there everyday, so accept it AND GO HAVE FUN. The world is your playground, Stevie. When life gets serious, go to the park and swing for a bit. While running errands, do some people watching and look for big smiles. When cleaning the house, turn the music up and dance. When you go to work, be grateful to have a job. However, if you are not appreciating the work you are doing, quit. Yes, quit. Do not spend a third of your life hating your career.

Look in the mirror often, Stevie. If you are not living, laughing, and loving the majority of your day, CHANGE IT! It is amazing to be alive. There is beauty that surrounds us everywhere – we just need to look.

Alright, let us get serious for a minute. Good. Now we can enjoy the remaining 23 hours and 59 minutes of today.

Lesson #64: One Hat Will Never Be Enough For Every Occasion

It will seem like as soon as you are able to speak, people will start asking what you want to be when you grow up. As soon as you start school, you will start being prepped to grow up and make something out of your life. Once high school is done you will be expected to get a job or start working towards a college degree. If you choose to go to college you will finish your classes in anticipation of starting a career. Wow, after rereading the last few sentences, Daddy is starting to wonder if it is worth teaching you how to talk!

Stevie, life is not about work. Life is not about what you do for a living. Life is not about how much money you make or what kind of car you drive. Yes, work is part of life. You will probably have many different jobs in order to make a living. It will be important to support yourself. What Daddy is trying to say is a job does not define who you are. You should not decide on a career based on the money you will earn. As you get older and through your adult years you will probably spend less than a third of your life working. That is a lot of time when you look at the big picture. Find work that you love and work with people you like. Find meaning in what you do and always work hard and be proud of your accomplishments.

Do not let your work define who you are but let your job be an extension of who you are. Be employed at a place where you can bring WHO YOU ARE to that job. Daddy loved being a bartender. He loves teaching scuba diving. He loves writing these lessons for you. He loves making people laugh. He loves being a good listener. He loves being a friend. He loves being a goof. Daddy loves being a Daddy and a husband. In life, we will wear many hats. If we have a hat that does not fit us anymore, well we can just get rid of that hat. The greatest thing about life is there are so many hats, if one does not fit, Daddy promises there are many more that will be perfect. Daddy plays in the ocean with other people who love the ocean. He shows people his love for the ocean. He writes to his little girl. It took a long time, but Daddy thinks he has got this work thing figured out. Here is a little secret Stevie, if he had to wear only one more hat for the rest of his life, the one that says Daddy would never leave his head.

Lesson #65: It Is Never Just A Kiss

Stevie, you are all about giving and receiving kisses recently. A kiss is the stuff that dreams are made of and the embrace which wakes up sleeping princes and princesses in fairytales. Kisses are the words that movies and plays are based on and make the heart skip some beats. The power of a kiss is electrifying. A kiss can be anticipated for hours or days and once delivered can be etched into our memory for a lifetime. A first kiss you will remember forever. A last kiss can sometimes say goodbye. Always remember to lean to the right when delivering a kiss on the cheek as a greeting to avoid an awkward moment. The power of a kiss on an injury? Daddy has never seen a boo-boo that did not feel better after a kiss. A kiss can send a wish on its way. A kiss can have you guessing for days and days. A kiss can make sure there are no monsters under the bed. The most powerful of all kisses is the one that lets you know that everything will be alright. Stevie, you will have a lifetime of many kisses. Each kiss will have a meaning, some more than others. Each kiss will be like a snowflake. A kiss is never just a kiss. A kiss is a little piece of magic. Some kisses you cannot define and those are the kisses that you will remember. Do not worry Stevie, you will never run out of kisses. You will have an endless supply. So why not give another one to Daddy?

Can you smell it, Stevie? Spring is in the air! We had another amazing Easter. Daddy added another year of sobriety to his tally. The Cubs are in sole possession of first place (wait let me double check...yep!). Grandpa tells us the snow is melting on the mainland. Kids are getting excited about summer break. The Blackhawks and the Bulls are in the playoffs. The Bears have high hopes on a new season. You just bounced back from your first really bad virus.

Lesson #66: Life Is Good

At some point in our lives, we are either taught or deem it socially acceptable to complain when asked simple questions like, "what is going on?" or "what is new?" Yes, Daddy can be guilty of this during the course of a conversation. This got me thinking, we all have so many things that are going right in our life, why not chat about those subjects? Why put the emphasis on what is going wrong? Why tell everyone who will listen about our aches and pains?

The other day Daddy had a light bulb moment. He was talking to a friend and they asked Daddy how he was doing. Guess what, Stevie? Daddy said, "I am doing really well." After Daddy hung up the phone, he sat there and thought about the conversation and realized something monumental. Daddy *was* good. For the first time in Daddy's life, he was *really* good. No complaining. No lying. No guilt. No aches or pains.

Life is good. Never has Daddy said that and felt like he was telling the truth. What an ah-ha moment.

This does not mean that things will not pop up that will upset Daddy. Or that there will be no more aches and pains. All this means is that there are ten things going right for every one thing that might be going wrong. Why not make a decision and focus on all the amazing things that are present? Daddy has tried to teach you to look in the mirror and love who you see. Today, Daddy can look in the mirror and know that life is really good.

Stevie, Daddy looked into your eyes many times this week and every time the answer was right there.

Lesson #67: Focus And You Will Find The Beauty In All Circumstances

Life will have bittersweet moments. We seem to grow so much more during these moments it is like we need these bumps and hiccups to keep us on the road of who we want to be. These impasses are when we find those ah-ha moments we talked about in our last lesson. There are times when we are in a relationship that is ending and it hurts badly. We can fool ourselves for months, weeks, or years in thinking that the bond is still strong and we need to stay in the relationship because it will be too painful if it ends. Then somehow the ah-ha moment happens, and we know we must leave in order to be happy. Sometimes we stay in a situation for security, even though the last thing we are feeling from it is secure. Then somehow we will have our ah-ha moment and we will understand we need to give up our security in order to really find freedom. We will stay in jobs, friendships, partnerships, even if we are being underappreciated because we want to avoid pain. We confuse being hurt with staying in a bad situation except the situation is screaming for the exact opposite. After we keep doing the same thing over and over again and expect different results but nothing different happens, eventually the ah-ha moment presents itself. Change can be scary. Stevie, how do you get through these bittersweet moments?

Sit down, relax, breathe, focus and you will see only you can stop the cycle. The pain will go away with time. AH-HA! Sit down, relax, breathe, focus, and be grateful that whatever the circumstance, you loved yourself enough to seize the moment. Cherish and love those times and then let them go. Life is full of so many beautiful things and even the most bittersweet moments have beauty surrounding their core. Sometimes you just need to sit down, relax, breathe, focus and find that beauty.

Daddy wanted to try and put a spin on something that is usually looked at in a negative way. You actually gave me this idea awhile ago but Daddy did not know how to incorporate your favorite thing into a lesson. Stevie, you have always loved your rocks. You love to collect them, carry them everywhere, and keep them safe.

Lesson #68: Sometimes The Best Place To Be Stuck Is With "Your Rock" And A Hard Place

You will hear the saying "stuck between a rock and a hard place" so many times in your life. Daddy can almost guarantee that every time you hear this, it will have a negative connotation. Let us start by looking at what a rock is in the first place. A rock is something physical and very hard to break. A rock will stay put where you place it and will always be in that spot when you need it. A rock can be big and heavy or small so you can carry it with you wherever you go. A rock can be built on, or used to build incredible things. A rock can keep you dry in the rain and you can skip it in the lake. What Daddy is trying to say is a rock is so much more than just a rock. In your lifetime, you will have many rocks. Daddy has had many rocks in his life, and has been a rock to a few others as well.

Stevie, when you are in a hard place, a rock can be a gift. Daddy has been very lucky to have had and still have some amazing rocks in his life. As you get older, seek out those rocks, love and appreciate those rocks. Be a rock to others. You will never be alone in a hard place, because you have two rocks in Daddy and Mommy.

Lesson #69: You Have The Most Amazing Life Coach Playing On Your Team

Daddy married up, and you, Stevie, got the number one draft pick. You scored the winningest coach of all time. When it comes to Mommies, you hit the megabucks lotto. Your Mommy was Colorado's best kept secret. Then she moved to Chicago and somehow swam under the radar long enough for Daddy meet her. One day you will have to ask Mommy how Daddy chased her around with an engagement ring begging her to put it on! Mommy is the perfect person for you to emulate. As Mommy grew up she looked inside herself and dealt with all life threw at her to become a better person. She is such a strong woman. Mommy loves herself. She hits all issues head on. Mommy knows how to forgive. She believes in and loves people. She laughs and love comes out. Mommy can make a house a home and understands the importance of family. She is a great listener. Mommy strives to be happy. She lives life now. She is open minded. Mommy stands up for herself and can take care of herself. She can also curse like a sailor!

As a matter of fact, you picked up one of Mommy's favorite words: O' Cean! (Or at least that is what we told you Mommy says…)

Mommy can make you feel safe with her words and will stand by her word. She has high morals and beliefs. Daddy has an amazing fear of an angry Mommy (he should probably take that out). Mommy will love through good and bad. She can toss a softball and nail a three-pointer. No stain can beat her. But the very best thing about Mommy is she loves with all her heart. If Daddy has one wish of what kind of woman to mirror, it would be your Mommy. Daddy could not have asked for a better wife, best friend, partner in crime, traveler, opponent, dive buddy, decorator, stylist, or mother for his daughter. As you get older, when life throws you offsides, ask yourself one simple question. What would Mommy do? Ninety percent of the time everything will work out for the best if you follow her lead. The other ten percent you will have a whole lot of fun figuring it out. Now Daddy has to go change his shirt before Mommy gets home. What are you laughing at, Stevie?

Happy Mothers Day, Natalie. We love you with everything we have over here. Thank you for all that you do, and thank you for all that you are.

Everyday you seem to be adding to your vocabulary. Daddy stares at you in awe each time a new word pops out of your mouth. Since you are getting older it is time to say goodbye to a very good friend that has always been there for you. This friend has comforted you, made it easier to sleep, and helps dry your tears. Daddy knows this will be very difficult, but it is almost that time.

Lesson #70: Bye-Bye, Paci

Stevie, as we get older we have a tendency to cling on to things we know. We want to keep things as they are because it is comfortable. We have a need to understand everything that we are doing. We want to feel safe at all times.

Your Paci has always been there for you. When Mommy and Daddy tucked you in at night, Paci stayed right there. When you were upset with Mommy and Daddy, Paci calmed you down. When Mommy and Daddy introduced you to all kinds of strangers, Paci stood in front of you with a watchful eye. Stevie, Daddy is going to fill you in on a little secret. You did all of this on your own. All of these changes you have underwent and through all of the uncertain times - you have been a big girl the whole time. It is time to say, "bye-bye, Paci." Stevie, it is okay to be uncomfortable because new desires will be born from that discomfort. Think of all the exciting things you can do instead. You can go to the park and meet new friends. Try singing out loud during bath time – it is liberating! If you try new things and you do not like them, you can always go back to what you know and love. Getting out of that Paci zone will help you open your eyes. It will introduce you to new and thrilling things. It will keep days from becoming ordinary because you ventured out into a new place. Live, Love, Laugh. Stevie, we will miss Paci, but know that you can always come back and see your old friend.

Today's lesson is very serious. Daddy wanted to wait until you were a bit older before laying this one on you.

Lesson #71: It Is Loyalty And Not An Obsession

Daddy has fought this fight all of his life. Daddy can also say he is probably loyal to a fault. Loyalty is such an amazing thing. Daddy has changed his mind about a lot of things as well, but in certain areas of life, has always remained loyal. Ask Mommy about Daddy's loyalty and she will probably roll her eyes and say something smart. Well, that is not really fair. He has slowly worked his magic on Mommy. Daddy thinks Mommy gets it now. He will teach you about loyalty as well, Stevie. You are part of him, so it will be easy to teach. Some days you will love your Daddy for teaching you this lesson on loyalty. Other days you may be angry. Sadness is a big part as well. Hope! There is hope! There will be tears shed but there is no turning back and that is okay. Do not be scared or confused. No matter what, Daddy will always be here for you as you learn to accept, grow, and deal with this obsession. There are others like us but they may not have the exact same loyalty issues we have. Daddy may look at them like they are fair-weather or disloyal, yet in the same breathe, Daddy understands them. You are old enough now, Stevie. When you scream out DA BEARS!, you are part of something big. You will never get to see Payton fly over the top, Big Cat Williams open up a hole, Doug Plank stop a receiver cold or Hampton and Dent make a sandwich out of a quarterback. This saddens Daddy, but knows you will have many new memories. There will be more great players that we will watch and cheer for together. We will always urge our team on, and hold our head up high. We will always be loyal to The Chicago Bears. Sunday will be here very soon. Stevie, are you ready for some football?

Daddy knows we are on holiday and no one wants to learn while on vacation. This lesson will be simple, but poignant.

Lesson #72: Life Is Happening Now

Wherever you go, whatever you do, however you look at it -- life is happening now. Be present, Stevie, and get all you can out of everyday. This one was short and sweet, just like you. Now, let us get back to our walk.

Stevie, your Daddy is another year older and still learning new and amazing things from you everyday.

Lesson #73: You Can Teach An Old Daddy New Tricks

Watching you learn new and exciting things everyday is so fun for Daddy. You have this cute way of staring at our lips to try and say new words. Without much thought, you race to new and exciting challenges. With eyes wide open, you look to Mommy and Daddy as if to say, "teach me." You study everything with the intention of gaining a new found skill.

When Daddy became sober, he looked back at how he treated and felt about himself, but only fully understood these changes when you were born. Since you came into his world, life has been fast. Everyday there are new things to learn and new ideas to explore. Everyday there are new sights, sounds, and emotions to see hear and feel. There are new lessons to be learned daily. Daddy thinks that he really started learning all over again when you came into his world. The most exciting part of all of this is that Mommy and Daddy get to do this with you. If he had you by his side in school, he probably would have a PhD. It does not matter how old you are, learning is fun as long as you allow yourself to be teachable.

Daddy is unsure if he ever said thank you for being the teacher of all of these lessons, and letting him learn as he goes. Thank you for opening Daddy up to amazing adventures. One day when you sit down and read all of these lessons Daddy wrote for you, know in your heart that you taught all these lessons to him as well.

Lesson #74: The Story Of Your Life

Stevie, there will be occasions when you are completely immersed in an experience and loving the moment. For some of these moments, you will not have a camera to take pictures. Take every moment that you want to capture and tuck it away.

Sometimes, the best moments do not need any words. They do not need a description. All they need is your mental snapshot remembering what you saw, felt, and heard. These moments strung together are the memories that will make up the story of your life.

Daddy keeps having the same dream over and over. You, Mommy and Daddy are all sitting on the beach and the wind is blowing lightly. The waves are hitting very softly and there is a low constant hum of the sea. The sun is just about to set and the sky is exploding with swirls of red, orange and yellow. Life is as it should be and for the first time there are no wants. Then Daddy wakes up from this incredible dream and starts the day. Today it hit Daddy. He has made this dream his reality.

Lesson #75: Dream Big!

Dream huge, Stevie, and then allow yourself to live what is in your imagination. Go after your dream career and be limitless as you are exploring your options. Take amazing care of yourself by loving who you are at the core. Give away love, with no strings attached. Take long trips to faraway places and enjoy all the steps of the journey.

Why should dreams be something you are only allowed to see when your eyes are shut? Focus on your desire, put in the work, and your dreams will come true. If you are working hard and your dreams are not manifesting, maybe it is time to look at your dreams. We can all say we want more money, but why not appreciate the things we currently have that provide comfort and support? We can all say we want a bigger house, but why not be grateful to have a place to lay our head? We can all say we want new toys, but why not give thanks that our bellies are full? We can all say we want to be loved, but why not start by loving and accepting ourselves? Dreams start to become a reality when you learn to love yourself, appreciate what you have, and you are grateful in the moment.

Daddy knows how blessed he truly is day after day. "Why," you ask, Stevie? It is really simple, my love. Daddy watches you playing with Mommy at the beach, which is the same thing he dreams about every night. Dreams do come true. He knows this because he gets to look at you everyday.

Today is Auntie Margaret's birthday, which is why today's lesson is so appropriate.

Lesson #76: Chance Encounters Can Be Gifts From Heaven

Every now and then the sea is nice and flat, the winds blow just right so the air is cool enough for a soft blanket, and the stars shine so very bright. Every now and then you will meet a complete stranger for just a brief moment. You will not know it then, but your life has been forever changed. Daddy thinks about chance meetings every time he reminisces about how he met Mommy. Through a glass window Daddy saw Mommy and BAM! He was knocked to the ground.

Daddy can also think about this the time he met Auntie Margaret on a long and very hot drive from Mozambique to Swaziland. The universe brought a stranger into Daddy's life that would one day give him the confidence to believe that these personal lessons to you should also be turned into a book so others can read and possibly benefit from them too. Daddy is grateful she was in that small, smelly, cramped bus in the middle of nowhere, yet exactly where he needed her to be.

These chance encounters will happen all throughout your life and each relationship, long or short, start out this way. Sometimes, they are just strangers passing in and out of your life with a smile and a hello. At other times, the rendezvous will result in a life long friendship filled with laughs and well kept secrets. Every meeting will come with a lesson if you allow yourself to be open and in the moment. You never know when a brief chance encounter will give such a blessed gift as a friend, a wife, or a daughter. It goes to show you how amazing and miraculous these meetings can be in your life. A conversation on a bus in Africa led to an amazing friendship. A simple look through a window planted a seed that became a family. Stevie, start with a chance encounter, and who knows, maybe the next thing you will be staring at is a sea full of love.

Stevie, we are having an absolutely beautiful day. It is hot and sunny, and the plumeria tree is blooming so there is a sweet smell in the air. The breeze is coming off the ocean cooling our warm heads. At this moment life is pure bliss. There is that word again -- moment. Moments seem to be in so many of our lessons and today is no different.

Lesson #77: How Can Life Be Bad When There Are Countless Perfect Moments Everyday?

No matter what is going on in your life, you can instantly get it back to perfect, even if only for a moment. If there are a gazillion curveballs being thrown at you, then you need to find those gazillion perfect moments to hit back.

Think about it, Stevie. Before you get out of bed in the morning, that first stretch feels so good. Stop and enjoy its simple splendor. That first cup of milk in the morning, or for Daddy, that first sip of coffee is sublime. Think about all the perfect moments already adding up and it is still only morning: a hot shower, the way your mouth tingles after you brush your teeth, a happy story on the news, and a quick kiss to Mommy before going to work.

Some of Daddy's favorite moments come from walks on the beach, a quick peek of a deer on the side of a road, money found in a winter coat. Let us not forget how great a baby's laugh sounds or the release of a long awaited sneeze or when all the green lights sync up as you are driving. The list can go on forever. We could do this all day and all night for weeks. There is an endless supply of perfect moments. They may last a brief second or a few hours, but in succession they are a lattice patchwork of joy.

Stevie, on those days when life seems to be beating you up, slow yourself down and look for one perfect moment. Once you find one, Daddy bets it is going to be really hard to not find another and another and another. As Daddy is typing this lesson, you are playing with your computer. You are trying to type just like him. What a perfect moment for him to take a quick peek at you. What an absolutely perfect moment.

Lesson #78: Life Is Not A Dress Rehearsal

This is your life, Stevie. Once today is over there is no going back so make today count. Make today meaningful. Live for right now, this very moment you are in. Love where you are and if you are not happy with where you are, change your course. Make phone calls and tell others you love them. Try to do one new thing everyday – even if it means walking home a different route or trying a new food. Buy yourself something nice and meet friends for dinner.

It is okay to be excited about the holidays in two months as long as you remember that there is a lot of life before that date arrives. We all say things like, "I can't wait until…" or "We are going to have so much fun next…" There is nothing wrong with that as long as we are just as excited about now!

This is not a dress rehearsal, Stevie. Make mistakes and learn from them. Meet new people and grow with them. Pack your bags and get stamps in your passport. You have one life and you should live it to the fullest extent. Thank you, Stevie. It took your birth for Daddy to fully grasp the full meaning of this lesson. You know what Daddy is excited about right now, Stevie? At this moment, he was able to share a bit of wisdom with his daughter, which she ingrained in him. What is Daddy excited about next? He does not know yet because he is still here, exactly where he should be!

Lesson #79: When You Do Not Think Twice About Sharing Your Chocolate Chip Cookie

Stevie, there will come a time in your life when everything will make complete sense. The moment when the first thought of the day is the exact same as the last thought of the day. You will learn there are many types of love. There is the type of love you have for Elmo and Cookie Monster. There is the type of love you have for a chocolate chip cookie. There is the type of love you have for going to the beach and running into the ocean. There is the type of love you have for a puppy or meow meow. Then, there is a love that blows all the others right out of the universe! It is a love you must put work into to make it flourish. The funny part is the simplicity in getting there: love yourself, forgive yourself when you make mistakes, take care of yourself. You will then be ready for and ready to share the most mind blowing, out of this world, Bears winning the Super Bowl love you have ever experienced.

Your partner is your co-pilot. You always can count on them as you go through the ups and downs together. Winning is about a game of Scrabble. Selfishness is about finding a way to spend more time with each other. Laughter is usually seconds away. Life does have a lottery and it does not revolve around money, power or fame. It is about the two of you, you and your soul mate, and when you get right down to it, that is all that matters. It is called unconditional love for a reason. It is the most amazing love you can experience. The biggest tsunami, the strongest earthquake, and the deepest freeze, cannot destroy it. It is about sitting on the beach, listening to Elmo songs, petting meow meow, and sharing your last chocolate chip cookie with the one you love.

Daddy cannot believe he has a two year old. What a great day we had yesterday celebrating your birthday! It seems like yesterday you were sleeping on Daddy's chest in the hospital, so fragile and small. Two years later and you have turned into such an amazing little girl. The last two years have flown by. When everyone sang Happy Birthday to you, it really hit Daddy that his baby was growing up so fast.

Lesson # 80: Let The Compliments Fly!

Birthdays are great. It is so nice to have so much attention directed at us, and have everybody saying such nice things about us. It is wonderful to feel so special. Why do we only seem to really let those compliments fly on someone's birthday? Stevie, tell people you love that you love and care for them often. Why? It is simple -- because it feels good!

It is amazing when a compliment make somebody's day. We get so caught up in ourselves at times that we seem to forget about others. Ask people about their day. Tell Mommy she looks beautiful. Notice a friend's new haircut. Inquire about people's hobbies. Ask, but even more important, listen.

Think about it, Stevie. How much better would life be if everyday we felt like it was our birthday? Did you notice all those smiles you saw all day? That is because it was a day to celebrate you. So, why stop at yesterday? You blow Daddy's mind. You light up a room with your smile and will turn anybody's bad day around. Your laugh melts Daddy's heart. You learn so quickly that he is convinced that you are a genius no matter what Google says. Your sense of style is impeccable; Mommy has taught you well (see what Daddy did there?) You give so much love away freely, which is how Daddy came up with this lesson. Keep letting the love fly!

Happy Birthday to my beautiful, smart, talented, funny, stubborn, loving, and sassy (Daddy could go on forever) daughter. Daddy loves you!

Daddy has been sitting out on the lanai while you were napping, thinking and enjoying the nice breeze. This has been a year full of loss. This year, Daddy has lost more people than in any other year he has been alive. Daddy is not sure if it is has just been an odd year or if it is because Daddy is getting older. You are two years old already, Stevie. It seems like just yesterday Daddy was writing Lesson number one. Time sure does fly by and the older you get, the quicker time will pass.

Lesson #81: Love Has No Expiration Date

As Daddy thought about all the people that have passed, he is not so much sad as he wishes he had one more moment with them. Daddy desires one more conversation, one more ball game to watch, one more lunch or one more sunset.

Losing people is a sad part of life but one that could be less painful if you took the time loving them when you had the moment.

Love has no expiration date. We love our loved ones, even when they are gone. That love never ceases and in some ways it even grows stronger. Do not waste a chance to tell somebody that you love them. Make plans to get together, and do not cancel. Do not get involved in the stuff that does not matter, because you miss all the stuff that does matter. At the end of the day, we should all be striving to do things that add quality to our lives. What did you do today?

One day you will read all of the lessons, and Daddy hopes you learn a bit, laugh a bit, and understand him better. You may be peeved with Daddy for sharing today's lesson with everybody. He can actually hear it now in his head, "Really Dad!" It is funny because in his head you sound like Mommy.

Lesson #82: It Is Time

There comes a point in life where you have to start taking care of yourself. You have had an amazing run so far - two full years. Starting tomorrow, we need you to focus and begin the process of learning to take care of yourself. Wait until you see the rewards that are going to start coming your way! There is no better feeling than looking in the mirror, loving what you see, and thinking, "I've got this!" That sounds easy, but for many of us life is a journey of learning, trying new things, making mistakes, succeeding, failing, loving, and letting go.

Tomorrow, you start a new adventure. Stevie, it is time to poop in the potty. There will be no more of wetting yourself. There will be no more of waiting in your own stink until you offend somebody enough to change you. There can be no more laying on your back, relaxing, while others tend to your special moments. And believe Daddy, you have had a lot of special moments. It is time you get a bit dirty. There will be accidents. There will be almost-made-its (hopefully Mommy will have most of these). There will be laundry. There will probably be crying...most likely coming from Daddy.

Through all of this Mommy and Daddy will be here praising, cheering, and celebrating you. For every successful triumph, we will do our version of an end zone dance. Daddy knows there will be moments of doubt and unease, but we will be by your side, so your front and back are clear. Tomorrow we shall go poopie and pottie in the potty! The numbers one and two will take on a brand new meaning. Tomorrow, Stevie will become a big girl! Next week, Daddy will go to the top of the volcano and scream, "my Stevie is potty trained!" Or at least that is what it looks like in his head. What he cannot wait to see is the look of pride in your eyes. The look that says, "Daddy, I've got this."

Lesson #83: Things We Do For Love

Daddy was forty years old when you were born. That means when you graduate high school, he will be fifty eight years old. Every time he thinks about that, it makes his head spin. Daddy and Mommy gave up good paying jobs to move to Hawaii. Every time Daddy looks at his paycheck it makes his head spin. Every time Daddy does something he should be able to do physically and grunts and groans, it makes his head spin. Yes, it is true, your Daddy is dizzy a lot. So now since we are all kinds of dizzy, let us throw in a dash of morbidity.

We lost Grandpa a few years ago and Grandma this year. Sprinkle in a bit of baldness and a teaspoon of weight gain. What do you get? Daddy's not getting any younger. Yet, he still has one heck of a personality! Then Mommy steps in and says, " time to make another baby."

Daddy starts sweating, shaking, worrying, and doubting. You will learn one day very soon, that. when Mommy's mind is made up and she speaks, it is better to just say okay. Stevie, you deserve a brother or sister. You deserve Mommy and Daddy to do all we can to give you a sibling who can be your best friend as you both grow up.

Daddy's not planning on going anywhere anytime soon, but it would have been selfish on Daddy's part not to give you a sibling. So, guess what? On May 3, yes Grandma's birthday, you will become a big sister! Thanks to Mommy and you, Daddy is different today than when you were in Mommy's belly. He is so excited to meet your brother or sister! Daddy cannot wait to add to our family. It is true, the things we do for love everyday is so amazing. Love is so powerful, that even when your head is spinning and your mind is screaming, "what are you crazy?!" your heart wins and everything is perfect. If you want an easy way to get through life Stevie, always do for love. If you do this, Daddy can pretty much promise you, it will be one amazing ride.

Lesson #84: There Is A Costume For Every Occasion

Yesterday, you were a cute bumble bee and last year you were a friendly ghost. Does that mean you have only worn two costumes so far in your whole two years? Absolutely not. Life can be like Halloween every single day. Think of all the characters real and imagined you have played in two years. You played a baby, a toddler, and now a little girl. You have been a student and a teacher. You are an amazing daughter and are preparing to become a big sister. You are a dancer, a cook, a comedian, a storyteller, a singer, and so much more. You have captained a boat. You have been a cowgirl. You have performed in movies. You have drawn portraits. You have been a niece, a cousin, a granddaughter, and a great granddaughter. How are you not exhausted!

Through all of these wardrobe changes, you have expressed so many emotions. You have brightened the days of so many people and made them laugh. As you get older, these characters will become more evolved and maybe a bit deeper. Some days these characters will be heavy or sad. Life is amazing, Stevie. The world we live and play in is incredible. Everyday we get to play so many different roles and put on numerous hats. Love these different costumes and embrace these different characters. Do Daddy a favor? ALWAYS BE YOU. Wear the hats, play the characters, and show off the costumes but through it all BE YOU.

Be true to who you are in all that you do. Halloween is for make-believe and is so much fun. Everyday life is reality and so much more breathtaking. BE YOU in everything you do. BE YOU in every role you play. BE YOU in every relationship you have. BE YOU in every situation that pops up. BE confident in who YOU are. BE proud of who YOU are. BE who YOU want to be. Why be YOU? Because, YOU are extraordinary. One more thing, Stevie, can Daddy see what kind of candy you have in that bag?

What a treat you gave Daddy the other night, Stevie! To see the circus through your eyes was incredible and left him a changed man again, thanks to you. Today's lesson is something Daddy needs to remember to go back to again and again.

Lesson # 85: When You Cannot Turn That Song Off

You have heard that circus theme song now, Stevie. That is the song that plays in Daddy's head on repeat when all the small things pile up and he thinks he has lost control or he cannot enjoy anything because he has to make it through the long to do list.

Da da dada dada da da da da da da dadadada…the circus takes on a negative connotation for Daddy and it does play in his head a lot. You will probably hear Daddy hum it many times.

There will be hard times in your life, Stevie. One day you may come home with a bad test score and feel awful. You might go in for a hair trim and leave with a pixie cut and be really angry. There will also be harder times. You may not get that job you really wanted and feel down. Your car may break down in a snowstorm and you are by yourself and feel scared. There will be the hardest of times. Some people you know may be going though a horrible illness and feel helpless. There might be a sudden loss of a family member or friend and you may question the existence of life.

That circus song will be so loud that your head will feel like it is going to explode. The despair, sadness and loneliness will be suffocating and the answers will be absolutely nowhere to be found. Here is the hard part, Stevie. Stop yourself, take a deep breath and remember these words: It is okay.

Daddy has a couple of sayings to keep close to your heart. Number one: we never have more than we can handle. This is so true! No matter what is going on, we can handle everything that is being lobbed our way. Number two: It is always working out. Even if you feel like the world is closing in on you, know deep in your core, that it will work out for you.

Daddy is going to keep this lesson in a visible place because he is stubborn and tends to forget these points. The real truth to this whole lesson is we do not give ourselves enough credit sometimes. We have an amazing ability to heal our hurt. If we can remember a couple of easy sayings it will make those times a lot more bearable. The funny thing about that circus theme song is when we hear it in our head, we forget just how much fun the circus is. Thank you for reminding Daddy that no matter how crazy life is, it is supposed to be fun. How does he know this? Because your laugh and smile turn any caterpillars Daddy finds into beautiful butterflies.

Lesson #86: We The People Can Be Awesome

Mommy laughs at Daddy all the time when he says he does not like people because of their objectionable behavior or actions. The truth is Daddy does not like all the ugly he sees in the world.

We tend to focus on so many depressing items it has a way of taking over our whole day. The news can be dreadful. We tend to complain about anything and everything. We can mistreat each other. We whine. We are never satisfied with what we have in our lives. We are jealous of others. We want and want and want! Some days the negativity seems just endless.

Then it happens, somehow the light enters the darkness inside. People throw fear out the window and accomplish what we were born to do. We allow in the love, even for just a minute, and something happens which brings out the awesome in people.

Today was one of those days, Stevie. A little boy has leukemia and only wanted one thing in life. He wanted to fight bad guys with Batman. Daddy knows that every kid wants to battle the villains with Batman; there is nothing original about that scenario. However the originality in this story came with what happened next. The city of San Francisco became Gotham City. The people of San Francisco became the cast of characters. The love of those people for that little boy became the story. And that little boy became a superhero. Daddy's eyes are pouring tears thinking about the pure beauty of this story.

When we put our minds to it, we can be wondrous. When we open up our hearts and let the love flow out, inspirational things happen. When we think of others before ourselves magnificence spreads. When we love and only love, well that is sublime.

Daddy has two friends who are twins and today is their birthday. Instead of cards or gifts they asked people to donate to the homeless. How cool is that? Excellence comes in all shapes and sizes. The San Francisco story was grandiose but we can keep it simple. Donate some time to a charity or pick up litter you see on the ground. Even smaller? Open the door for somebody. Be loyal, honest, caring and loving. Listen to a friend in need. Wrap your arms around a person and give a big hug. Put on a huge smile while doing jazz hands. Who does not smile and have their day brightened by jazz hands?

Find your awesomeness, Stevie, and give it to anybody who is willing to receive it. You have an endless supply of fabulous. Give it away and expect nothing in return and you know what? You will be surprised when you see all the awesomeness there is in the world just waiting to be seen. We are all capable of miracles but sometimes we need a reminder. Now smile, Stevie. Ready? Jazz hands!

Thanksgiving is Daddy's favorite holiday. Thanksgiving has a way of really making us look inside ourselves and allows this question to permeate.

Lesson #87: What Am I Thankful For?

It is a question we do not nearly ask ourselves enough, Stevie. If you want to be put into a good mood instantly, it is not any easier than asking this simple question -- what am I thankful for? If you are in a funk, you can ask yourself what you are thankful for today. If that is still not enough, you can ask yourself what you are thankful for right in this moment.

You do not believe me? Try it! A life fact is that if you think something will be easy it will, however if you think that it will be a struggle, then you will have to climb that mountain. The truth is, it is probably only a speed bump. The magic in the situation is your perspective on the matter. An easy way to gain perspective is to be grateful for the lesson you learned when the relationship ended or appreciate your abundant health even during the course of a cold. Appreciate the time you had with a person who just passed.

Daddy promises that on your very worst day, there will be something you are thankful for, Stevie. Life is amazing and beautiful. We are all so very blessed. At any given moment we can stop, take a deep breath, and ask ourselves, what are we thankful for? Daddy can look back at his life when he was doing anything and everything to screw it up and letting anger and fear control his life. You know what was missing from his life back then? This question. He never asked himself this simple question. Today Daddy asks himself this question so often that it is part of the DNA. On this Thanksgiving and every day after that, simply ask yourself this question. When times are tough, or for no reason at all, simply ask yourself this question. There is no better cure all for any misalignment than to focus on all the good things going on in your life.

Stevie, Daddy's superhero name for you is Smiley Girl! He loves this make-believe world you live in. The funny thing is Daddy truly believes you are a superhero. One day you will learn about real life heroes. One day you will learn about a real life hero that we lost today, Nelson Mandela.

Lesson #88: Wonder Woman Has Nothing On You

In your lifetime, you will see or learn about individuals that you will look up to. These people will show you that anything is possible. These people will show you that it is okay to dream big, and that those dreams can turn into reality. Daddy is not going to give you a long list of his heroes because Daddy wants you to find your own. One day we will talk about the people that have helped changed Daddy's way of thinking, feeling and living.

What is a hero, Stevie? Yes, you are right, Superman and Spider-man are superheroes -- but what really makes a hero? A hero faces fear and replaces it with hope. A hero takes the ordinary and strives for the extraordinary. A hero does not sit and watch injustice. A hero turns hate into love. A hero believes we are all equal. A hero wakes up everyday to inspire, love, teach, care, and help others for no other reason than it is in their heart to do so.

Stevie, Daddy thinks you are a superhero because you have the power to make anybody smile just by being you. As you get older, your might develop other superpowers. Here are some ways to fine tune your powers. Always show perseverance. Always believe in yourself and stand up for your beliefs. Continuously love and want better, not only for yourself, but for others as well. See the beauty in everything and everyone and sprinkle it around. Nelson Mandela said, "There is no passion to be found playing small - in settling for a life that is less than the one you are capable of living."

If we are born to love, then we are all born with the tools to be great people and there is no reason we cannot be super. We can then be heroes to others in the same way our heroes are inspirational to us. Let us go run those errands now Stevie, so I can watch your superpowers at work. I bet there are a few people out there that can use one of your smiles.

It is a boy! Stevie, you will soon be the big sister of your very own baby brother.
Daddy has no doubt that you are going to be an amazing big sister.

Lesson #89: Let The Games Begin!

The relationship you will have with your baby brother will be like no other, Stevie. You will now have a partner in crime to conspire with and drive Mommy and Daddy crazy. You will have someone to throw Mommy and Daddy off your trail when you make a mess. He can hear it now, "Brother did it, Daddy!"

You will have someone to explore magical worlds with and dress in costumes. You will have someone to look after and help pick up when he falls. The relationship between a brother and sister can be so unique. A simple look can express a thousand words which are unique only to you and your sibling. A few words can make the world make a bit more sense. A hug can remove you from a scary place to a place of warmth and safety. A brother-sister bond is sealed with love. There is nothing better than laughing for hours over the same old stories and nothing better than knowing you will be there to comfort each other through difficult times. You will have many friendships in your life Stevie, but none like the friendship you will have with your brother.

Mommy and Daddy hope your relationship is full of love. Stevie, make sure you guys know that you will always have each other's back. Stand up for each other. Every time you get uncomfortable about saying something to him, say it anyway. Make sure a day does not go by without you two knowing how much you love each other. Your baby brother is so blessed and he does not even know it yet. He has a big sister who showers the world with love everywhere she goes.

50

Daddy knows that your baby brother is going to do all right in this world because he has a big sister that is one heck of a teacher.

Tonight Santa comes after checking his naughty and nice list, Stevie. Daddy is sure that you made the amazing list. This magical time of year is a great chance to have a lesson about how things should be every single day.

Lesson 90: If We Can All Get Along On Christmas, Then We Can Do It The Rest Of The Year

Throughout Daddy's life, he has seen things that have confused him because he always tries to see the love in all situations. When Daddy hears jokes that start with a Jew, a Christian, and an Atheist walk into a bar, he would rather hear a story about three people who sat around and shared their beliefs. This is how it should be.

You may have a gay friend that is afraid to introduce her "special" friend to her family for fear of being disowned and shunned by the ones she loves. What Daddy would rather hear is about your gay friend who is nervous to introduce her girlfriend to her family because she wants her to be accepted and loved by her parents. This is how it should be.

The nation comes together and decides to elect the best person to run our affairs, and Democrats and Republicans collaborate together towards a uniformed goal. This is how it should be.

We look at the beauty of the world by the amazingness of the people who are living and loving each other. A place where we do not see the color of somebody's skin, but we do see the brightness of one's smile. This is so how it should be.

Tolerance is not a word we often use when we talk about our fellow men and women. Daddy was blessed to be raised around people with different backgrounds, religions, races and sexual orientations. He is able to see people based on who they are at their core, not their stereotype. This is how it should be. We all come from different roads and paths to get where we are and we all have amazing stories to share. We are all seeking the same things: happiness and love. This is how it is.

Daddy's ego has taken over this lesson by stating on how things should be. He is not trying to preach here, Stevie. Daddy wants you to walk your road, share your amazing stories, and treat people as you treat yourself. If we love and respect ourselves, it is so easy to pass the love we have onto others. So on this Christmas day and every other day, feel the spirit of the holiday and share your love with anybody and everybody, because this is how it should be. What is that, Stevie? Ha! Yes Stevie, even Packers fans!

Lesson #91: Make Room In Your Heart For A Little More Love

When the little guy comes into your world, things will definitely change. You will need to learn to be patient as you will be sharing space with your little brother. You will have to teach the dude all about sharing and making him feel welcome with your toys and books. You will have to let this alien explore your galaxy, as you teach him the traps and pitfalls of this brand new civilization he has come into. There will be days when you will feel like this is a burden that you did not sign up for and that you were wrongly drafted into this sibling army. There may be days when you feel like this creature was sent by The Dark Side to overthrow the grip you have around Daddy's pinky. Do not worry, Stevie! This might sound scary and overwhelming but in the end you will see that your heart will grow because of this little baby who has infiltrated your world. You will now have a partner who will follow you around with eyes opened wide in awe and wonder. You will have a friend you can confide in and a warrior you can lean on when you need strength.

Mommy and Daddy's heart expanded when you were born. You were our first little thing called love and we know from experience that when your baby brother is born, your heart too will swell so start making room for the love now.

Daddy loves introducing you to all different types of music. It is funny watching you try and figure out if you like a song. He is doing his best to keep you away from country music before Mommy gets her paws on you.

Lesson #92: Dance To The Beat Of YOUR Own Drum

Daddy loves all types of music, except country. It is funny but if he is sitting somewhere and country is playing in the background, Daddy actually starts getting angry. It sounds like it is not true Stevie, but if you ask your Mommy, she will confirm this craziness. Mommy loves country, and Daddy loves rock and roll. Mommy loves to dance, and Daddy likes to bob his head. Bands will release songs that make you dance all over the house, while other songs will make you run out of the room. Listen to music you like and dance to the music that moves you.

Music is a lot like life, Stevie. It is wise to invest time and energy in things that move you. Take classes that interest you, not the classes that only your friends are interested in. Read books which open your mind to new ideas and realms not only the books on your homework list. Find a job that fulfills and excites you and understand that the objective is not always about the big payday. Your lifestyle and your purpose are yours to decide. Form your own opinions and trust your own inner guidance to lead the way to your own happiness.

Life, like music, allows you to explore so very much, and there is so much to love about the variety.

It is so amazing to watch the little girl you are becoming. It is so much fun to watch your different emotions play out and show who you are becoming. Daddy watches your excitement when you make a new discovery. Your confidence grows every time you solve a problem. You have this cautious posture when you are a bit unsure of something. Daddy wants you to know that every emotion you feel is okay.

Lesson # 93: What Will Be Your Legacy?

It took Daddy a long time to really understand this lesson, Stevie. This lesson will change throughout your whole life, but the basic question and answer will always be the same. Right now, you are a carefree little girl with a huge personality. In a couple of years, you may be very curious student or one heck of a softball player. Down the road, you can be an Olympian!

This lesson is all about that very first lesson we talked a couple of moons ago. When Daddy looks in the mirror, he always strives to love the man looking back at him. His focus is about being the best father to you and your brother. Our legacies consist of things we put out in this world, and Daddy hopes that his legacy centers around the privilege it was to be a father.

As you get older Stevie, you will put some fantastic things out there. If you live life on your terms, your light will shine and your legacy will be bright.

Time for your check-up! Well Doc McStevie, you have been doing such an incredible job taking care of Mommy during her pregnancy. The amount of love and care you show makes Mommy and Daddy know that your brother is going to be one lucky kid. The way you love others at such a young age is amazing to witness. As you get older you are going to want to take the love you so freely give to others and give yourself a nice daily dose of it as well.

Lesson #94: Before You Point That Finger Somewhere Else, Point It At Yourself

As we get older Stevie, we are so quick to point the finger. You are just starting to learn this even at such a young age. If your friend was over, and your toys are all over the place you blame your friend for the messy room. Sometimes as we get older, we seem to pile the blame in the direction of everyone else, faster than a cheetah in action. We will leap over our part in a bad situation higher then a kangaroo. We will camouflage ourselves seamlessly to avoid the truth like an octopus. We will throw our friends, enemies, in-laws, co-workers, priest, and even our own mothers under a high speed bus before we will point that finger our way.

We will spend so much time pointing and preaching the fault of others, that we will leave ourselves exhausted from time to time. When you see yourself doing this Stevie, your pride is in need of a check-up. It takes so much less time and energy to point at yourself. Daddy is not saying that every time there is something wrong, it will be your fault. Most times when there is a problem, it is usually between two people. By looking in the mirror and taking responsibility for your part in a problem, that problem starts losing some of its flu-like symptoms. Every time we call ourselves out Stevie, we give ourselves a dose of healing medicine. We are not always perfect. We are going to say the wrong thing. We are going to hurt peoples feelings. We are going to mess things up. We are not always going to be understood. We are not always going to be right. And guess what Stevie, that is okay.

What can you do to try and heal up from these minor ailments? Treat the patient – you! It is easy and yet we make it so hard on ourselves. We stay healthy by treating ourselves well. When we point fingers we are not taking accountability for ourselves. Find out why that is and deal with the issues. That is how to live a healthy life.

Daddy knows that there are no rooms so messy that a little patience and work cannot clean them up. Daddy also knows Mommy and Daddy will always be here to help with those messy rooms. So, what do you say? Clean up, clean up, everybody, everywhere, clean up.

Why? Why? Why? This is your new favorite word, Stevie. Daddy loves your curiosity and as you get older you will ask more questions. Sometimes, you will be given answers that may make you ask even more questions.

Lesson # 95: It Is Always Okay To Ask Questions And Seek Out Your Truth

As amazing and as simple life can be, there are times when it will be confusing and anything but straightforward. Sometimes the answers to the questions are fairly obvious, while other times the answers will just lead to more questions. This is when you need to stop and do a simple thing we have talked about already and say, "It is okay."

There can be times when it will take awhile for the answers to reveal themselves to us. Sometimes, we are just not asking the right questions. Sometimes, we are asking the right question, just not in the right way. There will be instances when the answer is not what we want to hear. There will be other times we get an answer that we do not understand because we do not want to see the truth behind the answer.

While all of this sounds confusing, as long as you remember to keep asking the questions while searching for your answers, you will be just fine. Sometimes it just takes us a little longer to get to where we are going. Every now and then we need to stop asking, sit on answer that was given, and then see if we got our answer. There is no right or wrong way in finding your truth, as long as you are being honest with yourself. Daddy loves when you ask why and you stump him. This usually happens when Daddy is in a rush to do something else. Daddy needs to learn how to listen to your questions and process them. When he does not have the answer, he needs to take the time to meditate on the question. Answering your question might take a little time and some back and forth with you, Stevie, and that it is okay.

No matter how busy we are and Daddy is freaking out because there is never enough time, Mommy always keeps calm and exudes a quiet strength that is incredible to witness. One day Mommy will teach you how to remain composed and flexible to get through any obstacle. Until then, Daddy will try and take a stab at it.

Lesson #96: Girls Are Better Than Boys (SHHH!)

Daddy can see the look on Mommy's face now, "What are you teaching our daughter!?" Mommy did not like it when Daddy taught you to say "boys…bleh." Since we are so close to having your baby brother, Daddy needs to keep this lesson on the down low. This will be our little secret.

Let us break down the reasons why in many instances girls may seem to be superior to boys…bleh. As a girl, you hold a power over a boy by being right ninety nine percent of the time. The one percent of the time you are wrong is because you will show compassion and allow a boy to be right every now and then (or at least let them believe they are right).

Next, a girl sees that a house is so much more than a couch, a bed and a TV. Girls bring in REAL dishes and throw out the paper plates. They buy pillows that will never be used, but will add coziness to the couch. Girls will hang towels that are never to be used, but will be decorative pieces to make the room pop. They will hang pictures, mirrors, and place knick-knacks everywhere. A girl's inherent nature will turn a space into a home.

Only a girl understands that certain colors do not EVER go with others. Here is a real life example. Daddy will show Mommy the outfit he picked out and Mommy will shoot him a look. Daddy will throw his hands in the air while Mommy grabs the perfect shirt to assist him in not looking like a clown. Sometimes, Mommy will put out an outfit days in advance to avoid a Daddy fashion disaster.

Girls will take the time to smell pretty and look unwrinkled. Boys…bleh will hopefully shower and smell their shirt before putting it on. Not all boys…bleh will be dirty and not all girls will know what color shorts go with a fuchsia top. Daddy is using these caveman stereotypes to show you everything that Mommy did for Daddy. Mommy took a boy… bleh and helped him evolve into a man.

Boys…bleh have a lot of amazing qualities. Girls have a lot of amazing qualities. Even in each other's differences incredible things are created and both parties grow. Daddy will teach this lesson in the same way to your brother. Daddy will tell your brother all of the way girls will drive him crazy, but in the end how much he will love the challenges.

Stevie, Daddy saved the best part of this lesson for last. Why are girls better than boys…bleh? Simple, girls bring life into the world. Yes, you need a boy…bleh for this as well, but girls grow and care for a baby inside of them for ten months. If the roles were reversed, civilization may have ended as quickly as it started. To be a girl is such an amazing gift, with so many remarkable experiences which are unique to girls.

Seeing a girl turn into a woman and a boy…bleh turn into a man is what make life so enormous. Stevie, love being a girl. Love the process of growing into a woman. When you turn thirty seven, enjoy watching your boy…bleh turn into a man in the same way your Mommy enjoyed opening Daddy's eyes to so much more beauty. She helped shift the way Daddy saw the world on so many subjects. That is the power of love. Daddy thinks he had that effect on Mommy as well.

That is why when it is your brother's turn for this lesson, Daddy thinks he can give a couple of reasons why boys...bleh are better than girls.

Life seems to have been turned upside down a little bit, Stevie. Your brother Briggs finally made his appearance which has brought on a bit of an earthquake in our home.

Lesson #97: Change Is What We Decide To Make Of It

You want to change life as you know it? Have a baby! Want to really shake your world up? Have a second child! Going from a family of three to a family of four has been a juggle, right, Stevie? It all has to do with change and how we look at it, right? Throughout your life, you will go through lots and lots of changes. Some changes will be good, others will be great, some will be no big deal and others will be life altering.

You may become a person who does not like change or is scared of transition Or, you may be the opposite, and love change and strive for diversity. Daddy has been on both sides of change. Almost always, change is good. Then there are times when it can be bad. How do take the bad feeling and change it to a better feeling? When you can answer that question it will make your life so much more fulfilling

The reason why change can sometimes feel bad is pretty simple but yet we make it complex.

Change can be scary and make us feel lonely. Change can force us to leave the ones we love. Change can be uncertain and uncomfortable. Wow, change can be so many things! What else can it be? Well Stevie, change can be exciting. Change can allow us to meet new faces. Change can make time for us to see the ones we love. Change can be a learning and growing experience. See what we're getting at here, Stevie?

Change is what we decide to make of it. If we get right down to it, anything and everything in life can be good or bad right? A rotten banana can be yucky or used to make a delicious banana bread. A rainy day can be depressing or a day to go jump and play in the puddles. A new baby brother can be a pest that steals Mommy and Daddy away or be your new best friend. It is all how we choose to look at things. It is so easy to look at the bad in life and pull up a "pity pot". Why is this, Stevie? Daddy cannot answer that question because he is very guilty of this as well. It is so strange the work it takes to be happy. The work is to see the forest through the trees. We can all stare at the ocean and see the beauty. We can all see an old couple holding hands and see the love. We all have to work to see the beauty in the mirror. Accepting change as part of life is the start. Accepting change to grow and become an even more amazing person is the process. Accepting change and finding the good in everything is the main goal. What do you win, Stevie? That person in the mirror looking back at you and loving what they see.

Daddy and Mommy have an endless supply of love for you and with these all of changes, received another endless supply for Briggs too. What happens if it runs out? Inconceivable! Speaking of changing…wanna go get Daddy a clean diaper?

What is important in life, Stevie? Right now for you it is Frozen, milk, and Play Dough. A few months ago it was Elmo, your Paci, and puzzles. What life altering things will be important next, Stevie? Daddy thinks it may be school, new friends, and the park.

Lesson #98: There Is Only One Thing In Life That Is Important

You are going to go through so many changes in your life, Stevie. Some are going to be small and subtle, some will be life changing. As you get older and all of these changes take place, so will what is important. Everything that you know and love right now is simple. It is amazing to watch it through Daddy's eyes. You are so young and innocent and life is simple. Daddy hopes it stays that way for you for a very long time.

What is important to us changes as we get older. We start to want things that really have nothing to do with what is really important. We start to have responsibilities that we allow to overshadow what is important.

So, what is important in life? The answer is so simple. We can and do complicate it, but for right now let us put it in three easy words: OUR OWN HAPPINESS.

That is the simple, pure, uncomplicated truth. Milk makes Stevie happy. Going to the park makes Stevie happy. Laughing with Mommy and Briggs makes Stevie happy. So simple. Why do we lose some of that with time? As we get older we take the simplicity out of just being happy. Taking care of ourselves comes with responsibility and providing for ourselves. We feel that certain things become important Here is where the problem starts. Our wants become greedy, compulsive, hard to achieve, and less about us. Our wants become more about how we are perceived than who we are.

Is it nice to have a new car, Stevie? Yes absolutely, but it is better to have an adventure in that car. Is it nice to have a big house? Yes, but it is a lot better to have a loving home. Is it nice to have lots and lots of toys? Yes, but it is even more amazing to have friends to go out and play with. Daddy spent a huge part of his life arguing with himself and others about how happy he was. He spent a long time lying to himself about what it was that made himself happy. He did everything he could for a very long time to destroy everything that made him happy in his life. Daddy knows that sounds horrible but he did not keep it simple. He did not keep it innocent. Luckily he figured out a way to put that ego aside. Daddy figured out a way to be nice to himself. Most of all he figured out a way to forgive himself, and then the healing began. Daddy learned to love himself, and then the happiness came back. Then the magic happened.

Daddy met Mommy and won her heart. Then you came and filled Daddy with a love that he never knew existed. Daddy now has a job whose currency is love and has made him a rich man. Finally Briggs showed up to complete a family that can turn any house into a home and any trip into an adventure. Simply put Daddy knows today the true definition of what is important. As you get older Stevie, ask yourself this simple question. Am I Happy? If you do not immediately answer yes then stop, take a deep breath, and find the simplest thing that makes you happy and build from there. If you get stuck, call Mommy and Daddy. We will sit down, have a glass of milk and play with some Play Dough until we figure things out.

Stevie, the best part of Daddy's day is when you talk story. You can go on and on for hours (you get that from Mommy). Everyday you are learning and using new words at such a rapid pace. You will say a word and Daddy will just shake his head and wonder where you picked it up.

Lesson #99: Your Voice Will Be Your Greatest Tool

As you get older being able to speak takes on totally new meaning. Your words can make somebody feel loved, and at the same time can cut somebody like a knife. You can make people laugh with a simple joke, or cry with a heart felt toast. You can end a feud that has lasted years with just a couple of thoughtful words. You can destroy a relationship that has lasted years, with just a couple of spiteful words. Two phrases that you must learn to use because you will need to many times in your life are "I'm sorry" and "I was wrong". These two simple phrases become increasingly harder for some people to use as they get older. You are not always perfect, Stevie, nor should you try or expect to be perfect. That is why you will need theses two phrases throughout your life. A simple apology that is heartfelt will save friendships. A simple acceptance of blame will make you a better person.

Thank you, please, you are welcome, excuse me and hi are words that you should use everyday that ends in a Y. Use your voice to stand up for yourself when you are feeling misunderstood. Use your voice to make your feelings heard, when you are feeling mistreated. You will learn lots of words that have no business ever being part of your vocabulary. There are four letter words that you will think are so cool to use when you are younger, and as you get older and more mature will realize that they are not that cool. Except fart, because everybody loves the word fart.

There are words that will describe people in horrible and mean ways. Learn these words so you can use your voice to take away the power from these words. A word is simply put a word. How that word is used, and the power of that word will depend on how you choose to use it. Your voice can take away the bite of any mean nasty word. Use your voice for spreading the good and positive. Save your voice from spreading the gossip and the rumors. An old saying is, if you do not have anything nice to say, do not say anything at all. This is so true. Use your voice to sing, laugh, woo-hoo, teach, console, comfort, or just get to know someone. Use your voice to fight for what is right. Fight to be heard. Fight to be understood. The most powerful phrase you will ever voice is just three small words. I Love You. Three words that put together will have a million different meanings. Do not be greedy with these three words, Stevie. Tell the ones you love that you love them. Use these three words to make somebody's day. Scream them so loud that everybody in earshot hears. Whisper them as a private moment of encouragement. I love you. No three words together can be more powerful.

Stevie, Daddy just thought of something. Come closer. Closer. Gimme your ear…I love you. Wow, look at that smile. Yup three simple words, that make the world go around.

Well here we are Stevie, Lesson #100. What a journey of self-discovery this has been for Daddy. Daddy likes to think that he has taught you a lot in these lessons, but the real truth is Daddy was also learning as the lessons were being put to paper. Through all the previous 99 lessons one thing has been constant so let us keep that common theme.

Lesson #100: Every Life Lesson Will Always Start And End With Lesson #1

Lesson #1 says it all: always love who you see in the mirror. This is not a lesson of ego or conceit. This is a lesson of being true to you. If you do not love yourself, how can you ever love someone else? Loving yourself is not about a false character or alter ego that you create to shelter yourself from feeling. Loving yourself does not mean that you will not ever be upset with yourself. Loving yourself means being honest with yourself. You must be able to call yourself out. This is a hard one, Stevie. We do not ever like to be wrong, but guess what? It happens. We need to be able to look at ourselves and say we messed up. It is okay that we do not have all the answers, and we do not need to make up answers to be right. A sign of loving yourself is being able to learn from your mistakes. People who love themselves are able to forgive themselves.

This is so huge in self-discovery. Self-discovery is essential in living a full and happy life. The more you understand your desires, the easier it is for you to fulfill them. You may hear how much so and so loves themselves. This will be said with all sorts of negativity. When people are "arrogant", "stuck up" and "conceited" there is probably a lot more going on there than loving themselves. We create these personalities as to not hold ourselves accountable. Daddy was notorious for this for the majority of his life. Daddy to this day can find some of those old "friends" of his that are sometimes all too comfortable. That is the problem with not being true to yourself. You start to rely on these people you make yourself up to be.

It will not always be easy to look in the mirror and say that you love yourself. This is when you must. These are the most important times of self-discovery. Allow yourself to feel what you are feeling. Take the time to figure out why you are feeling a certain way. Allow yourself to feel that way without judgment. Before you know it, the answers to what is really important will present themselves. Be hard on yourself when the situation warrants. We so often give ourselves a free pass for our thoughts, feelings, and behaviors. Why? How are we going to grow and become the best us if we are always making excuses for ourselves? Through all of this Stevie, live your life knowing that you do not have to always be perfect. You do not have to have all the answers. You are allowed to mess up and make mistakes. You are not always going to say the right things. You are not always going to be understood or understand. Life is full of hiccups and "o' cean" moments, but you will be able to handle them. No matter how crazy life seems, take the time to breathe, sit still, and look in the mirror. If you love yourself, and are good to yourself the answers will come. If they do not come, there is your answer. Put the time in and search deep. Do the best that you can, and allow yourself to be honest and grow. Most of all, BE GOOD TO YOU. If you ever get stuck or lost and you need a bit of help finding your way back, come see Daddy. We will look in that mirror together, and before you know it, we will find that love.

Printed in the United States
By Bookmasters